AF888970

China in the World Economy: The Domestic Policy Challenges

SYNTHESIS REPORT

OECD

ORGANISATION FOR ECONOMIC CO-OPERATION AND DEVELOPMENT

ORGANISATION FOR ECONOMIC CO-OPERATION AND DEVELOPMENT

Pursuant to Article 1 of the Convention signed in Paris on 14th December 1960, and which came into force on 30th September 1961, the Organisation for Economic Co-operation and Development (OECD) shall promote policies designed:

- to achieve the highest sustainable economic growth and employment and a rising standard of living in Member countries, while maintaining financial stability, and thus to contribute to the development of the world economy;
- to contribute to sound economic expansion in Member as well as non-member countries in the process of economic development; and
- to contribute to the expansion of world trade on a multilateral, non-discriminatory basis in accordance with international obligations.

The original Member countries of the OECD are Austria, Belgium, Canada, Denmark, France, Germany, Greece, Iceland, Ireland, Italy, Luxembourg, the Netherlands, Norway, Portugal, Spain, Sweden, Switzerland, Turkey, the United Kingdom and the United States. The following countries became Members subsequently through accession at the dates indicated hereafter: Japan (28th April 1964), Finland (28th January 1969), Australia (7th June 1971), New Zealand (29th May 1973), Mexico (18th May 1994), the Czech Republic (21st December 1995), Hungary (7th May 1996), Poland (22nd November 1996), Korea (12th December 1996) and the Slovak Republic (14h December 2000). The Commission of the European Communities takes part in the work of the OECD (Article 13 of the OECD Convention).

OECD CENTRE FOR CO-OPERATION WITH NON-MEMBERS

The OECD Centre for Co-operation with Non-Members (CCNM) promotes and co-ordinates OECD's policy dialogue and co-operation with economies outside the OECD area. The OECD currently maintains policy co-operation with approximately 70 non-Member economies.

The essence of CCNM co-operative programmes with non-Members is to make the rich and varied assets of the OECD available beyond its current Membership to interested non-Members. For example, the OECD's unique co-operative working methods that have been developed over many years; a stock of best practices across all areas of public policy experiences among Members; on-going policy dialogue among senior representatives from capitals, reinforced by reciprocal peer pressure; and the capacity to address interdisciplinary issues. All of this is supported by a rich historical database and strong analytical capacity within the Secretariat. Likewise, Member countries benefit from the exchange of experience with experts and officials from non-Member economies.

The CCNM's programmes cover the major policy areas of OECD expertise that are of mutual interest to non-Members. These include: economic monitoring, structural adjustment through sectoral policies, trade policy, international investment, financial sector reform, international taxation, environment, agriculture, labour market, education and social policy, as well as innovation and technological policy development

Publié en français sous le titre :

La Chine dans l'économie mondiale : les enjeux de politique économique intérieure
RAPPORT DE SYNTHÈSE

© OECD 2002
Permission to reproduce a portion of this work for non-commercial purposes or classroom use should be obtained through the Centre français d'exploitation du droit de copie (CFC), 20, rue des Grands-Augustins, 75006 Paris, France, tel. (33-1) 44 07 47 70, fax (33-1) 46 34 67 19, for every country except the United States. In the United States permission should be obtained through the Copyright Clearance Center, Customer Service, (508)750-8400, 222 Rosewood Drive, Danvers, MA 01923 USA, or CCC Online: *www.copyright.com*. All other applications for permission to reproduce or translate all or part of this book should be made to OECD Publications, 2, rue André-Pascal, 75775 Paris Cedex 16, France.

Foreword

To reap the full benefits of further integration in the world economy, the Chinese economy must undergo fundamental adjustments. A substantial reallocation of resources among economic sectors and a major restructuring of the business sector will be needed to correct widespread inefficiencies. The government will face demands from society to ease the pressures created by this historic transition.

Many OECD Member countries which have undergone similar economic upheavals have found that international co-operation in the framework of the OECD can provide valuable support in designing institutions and policies that maximise the benefits of liberalisation while minimising its costs. This landmark study grew out of what the OECD perceived as a strong interest by the Chinese authorities in sharing the collective knowledge and experiences of economic development that OECD Member countries have accumulated through this process.

Since 1995, China and the OECD have engaged in a fruitful dialogue on many policy issues of common interest in the framework of a comprehensive programme of co-operation managed by the Centre for Co-operation with Non-Members.

This study takes stock of the results of these activities and develops the analysis of the policies that will have to be adjusted in order to meet the challenges of further trade and investment liberalisation. It is published under my responsibility.

I hope that this work can provide the Chinese authorities and people with tools and encouragement to continue their momentous undertaking.

Donald J. Johnston
Secretary-General
OECD

© OECD 2002

About the synthesis report

This is the synthesis report of a large study undertaken by the OECD Secretariat. It was written by Charles Pigott, Senior Economist, Economics Department, OECD, on the basis of the 22 chapters of the full study. The full study (see below) will be available in a separate volume.

About the study

This study has been undertaken in the framework of the ongoing OECD-China programme of dialogue and co-operation, managed on the OECD side by the Centre for Co-operation with Non-Members. Policy issues covered under the programme include tax policy, statistics, environment policies and indicators, agriculture, competition, enterprise reform, corporate governance, financial sector reform, insurance, education, and science and technology. Although the study draws on the understanding gained from several years of dialogue with a number of Chinese Ministries and Agencies, this remains an independent study of the OECD Secretariat.

Acknowledgements

This study has been produced by a cross-Directorate team led by Charles Pigott (Senior Economist for China in the Economics Department) under the supervision of Silvana Malle (Head of the Non-Member Economies Division) and has been co-ordinated by Frédéric Langer (Head of the China and Asia Unit of the OECD Centre for Co-operation with Non-Members).

OECD Contributors: Jón Blöndal, Peter Börkey, Sang Mok Choi, Andrzej Kwiecinski, Christina Tebar-Less, George Holliday, Marie-France Houde, Bernard Hugonnier, Xiande Li, Marie-Ange Maurice, Krzysztof Michalak, Elena Miteva, Makoto Nakagawa, Young-Sook Nam, Stilpon Nestor, Charles Pigott, Anders Reutersward, Udo Pretschker, Sally Van Siclen, John Thompson, Peter Whiteford, Terry Winslow, Aki Yamaguchi, Gang Zhang.

Outside Contributors: Chunlai Chen, Hunter Colby, Sylvie Demurger, Gerry Dickinson, Jean-François Huchet, Scott Jacobs, Gilles Lelong, Shantong Li, Wayne Morrison, Albert Park, Scott Rozelle, Jian-Guang Shen, Qihong Sun, Cunzhi Wan, Wei Wang, Shiqiu Zhang, Zhujian Zhou.

Research support: Chuen-Mui Wu Final copy editor: Kathleen Gray

The CCNM wishes to thank the experts from OECD Member countries and China who participated in the informal seminar under the auspices of the Economic and Development Review Committee on 10 December 2001 in Paris, contributing important comments on the draft study results. Experts from China, who took part in their personal capacity, were Mr. Wen Hai, Deputy Director, China Centre for economic research, Beijing University, Mr. Jun Han, Director General, Research Department on the rural economy, Development Research Center of the State Council (DRC), Mr. Kang Jia, Director, Institute of Fiscal Science, and Mrs. Shantong Li, Director General, Department of Development Strategy, DRC.

© OECD 2002

Synthesis of the Main Findings of the Study

China's progress during the economic reform era that began in 1978 has been one of the great economic success stories of the post-war era. China has become the world's seventh largest economy and second largest recipient of foreign direct investment. Only Japan and Korea achieved a comparable record of sustained rapid growth during the latter half of the 20th century. China's performance is all the more remarkable in that its reforms have been gradual and its development has occurred despite extensive, though declining, state ownership and intervention in the economy.

The accession of China to the World Trade Organisation (WTO) marks an important milestone along the reform path China has been following for more than twenty years, rather than a new direction. China has been liberalising its international trade and investment policies since the mid-1980s and is now as open as some present WTO members. Although China stands to gain significantly from the opening of its export markets under the terms of its accession, the depth and breadth of its commitments to liberalise access to its domestic economy are acknowledged to be more extensive than those agreed to by previous adherents to the WTO. This willingness reflects the fact that opening to international markets promotes market discipline, access to technology, and other qualities that have been important goals of domestic economic reforms. In this respect, WTO entry is a complementary aspect of the next phase of China's reforms.

This report synthesises the main findings and recommendations of the OECD horizontal study of the domestic economic policy challenges posed by China's further trade and investment liberalisation (TIL). The study comprises 22 detailed reports prepared by nine OECD directorates covering the adjustments and policy challenges facing the key sectors of the real economy over the next decade, and their implications for the policies that will be critical to success in meeting these challenges. The study represents an OECD perspective drawn from the experiences of its Member countries with economic transformations, and from the work of the OECD with China and other emerging economies over the past decade. The basic question the study addresses is: how can China best reap the benefits of its opening and other economic reforms over the next decade in order to meet its basic development objectives? The reports analyse the current problems impeding China's economic

© OECD 2002

development and identify key priorities and objectives, along with some suggested specific steps, in order to maximise the benefits of China's opening and other reform efforts. These analyses highlight the interdependence, and increasing need for co-ordination of policies in different areas.

Messages

The studies document the impressive progress China has made in transforming its economy during the reform era. At the same time, they indicate that the important engines that have driven China's growth in the past are losing their dynamism. The main reason is that China's economy has become badly fragmented and segmented, and this has led to increasing-under and inefficient utilisation of resources. Trade and investment liberalisation, although it will require difficult adjustments by some segments of the economy, will stimulate other segments and bring positive net benefits to the economy as a whole over the longer-term. However by itself, trade and investment liberalisation is unlikely to solve the basic problems now impeding China's economic development.

As it has throughout the reform era, the realisation of China's economic potential, including the full benefits of trade and investment liberalisation, rests on its success in continuing and strengthening its domestic economic reforms. However China's economy has reached a stage that calls for some important changes in the way economic reforms are carried out. As the economy has become increasingly exposed to market forces and the scope for self-contained development of individual sectors has declined, economic problems have become more and more interdependent. Conditions in particular segments of the economy, such as rural labour markets, industry, the financial system, and regional development, now depend as much or more on developments in other areas of the economy than on developments or policies in that specific segment. Economic distinctions among various parts of the economy that have been accorded different treatment are breaking down. This interdependence has led to several "vicious circles" in which problems in a number of areas interact in a mutually reinforcing fashion to impede progress in the overall reform process. Particularly difficult is the vicious circle involving the weak performance of many of China's enterprises and the problems of the banking system that is described in the next section.

In China's present situation, the outcomes of particular reforms depend increasingly on the interaction among measures taken by the economy's key actors – government, enterprises, workers, and the financial system – acting in markets whose functioning is shaped by key framework conditions such as competition, property rights, and corporate governance. Rather than emphasising particular sectors, reforms now need to focus more on *economy-wide* policies to promote more efficient allocation of resources and to bolster the effectiveness of markets. The study highlights three objectives as the key to the success of China's overall reforms over the next decade.

© OECD 2002

- The first and most immediate is to lay the foundation for improving the utilisation of China's resources, by removing present obstacles to business sector restructuring and by achieving better integration among various segments of the economy that have been developed separately under different sets of rules.
- The second is to improve competition law, property rights, enterprise governance and other frameworks that are essential to efficient market functioning so that resources are efficiently allocated in the future.
- And the third is to improve the capacity of the government to support economic development, by strengthening the effectiveness of macroeconomic policies while refocusing the role of regulatory policy on establishing and enforcing rules for market behaviour.

In achieving these objectives, reforms need to be both concurrent and carefully sequenced. Individual reforms to address particular problems need to be accompanied by complementary reforms in other areas in a comprehensive and co-ordinated fashion that is mutually reinforcing. Preferential development of individual sectors to "lead" the overall economy is likely to have much lower payoffs than in the past, and pose greater risks of negative outcomes. At the same time, reforms cannot be made all at once and care needs to be taken to establish the pre-conditions needed for follow-up measures.

Both principles will be particularly important to the achievement of three objectives which the study identifies as needed to break through the vicious circles now impeding reforms and establish the pre-conditions for sustained progress in the future. These are to:

- restore solvency to the financial system;
- bolster market based mechanisms as the dominant force for restructuring of the business sector;
- and establish public finances on a sound and sustainable basis.

Taking stock: the progress that has been made and the problems that need to be overcome

China's economy has undergone extensive transformations over the past twenty years (Table 1). The characteristic feature of the government's economic strategy has been to create separate channels for development outside the state sector, operating under different rules and conditions, in order to progressively increase the scope for market forces while phasing out central planning. This process, which has been termed "growing out of the plan",[1] has been highly successful but it has become increasingly apparent that its ability to push China's economic development further is coming to an end. Structural problems in

© OECD 2002

Table 1. **The transformation in China's economy**

	1980	2000
GDP per capita[1]	168	727[2]
Percentage of population in urban areas	20	31
Share of GDP (per cent) in:		
Agriculture	30	16
Industry	49	51
Services	21	33
Share of employment in:		
Agriculture	69	50
Industry	18	23
Services	13	27
Trade/GDP (%)[3]	12	42

1. In constant 1995 US$.
2. Figure is for 1998.
3. Exports plus imports as share of GDP.

Sources: World Bank, *World Development Indicators*, 2000; *China Statistical Yearbook*, 2000; IMF, *International Financial Statistics*. Figures for shares in GDP and employment for 2000 are from Chapter 1, Table 1.1.

Figure 1. **Real GDP growth**
3 year moving average

Source: China Statistical Yearbook, 2000.

© OECD 2002

the real economy have worsened progressively during the 1990s, leading to growing under-utilisation of labour and a protracted slowdown in real growth (Figure 1). These structural problems are substantially attributable to a lack of integration in factor markets, among business segments, and among regions.

Obstacles to resource utilisation in the rural economy[2]

China's agriculture employs about 50 per cent of the country's workforce and is characterised by relatively scarce land in relation to labour and small-scale production using little mechanisation. As in Japan and Korea, output per unit of land is high by international standards but output per worker is low. Land-intensive crops, notably wheat, corn, soybeans, and cotton are produced mainly in the northern part of the country while most of China's rice and sugar crops are produced in the southern half. Cultivation of vegetables, which are labour-intensive, is concentrated in coastal provinces and in areas adjacent to cities. Meat production is more evenly dispersed and largely carried out in small "backyard" facilities. Agriculture supplies less than half of total rural income. Per-capita incomes of rural households are 40 per cent of those in urban areas and, due largely to greater access to off-farm jobs, are highest in coastal areas.

Policy toward the rural economy continues to be carried out under frameworks and institutions distinct from those governing other parts of the economy. The Ministry of Agriculture is responsible not only for agricultural activities but also for general oversight of township and village enterprises (TVEs). The property rights regime in rural areas, in which village collectives formally own agricultural land, is distinct from that applying in urban areas. China's population registry system (*hukou*) includes provisions that impede migration of rural-born workers by preventing them from becoming legal residents of cities. Education resources per-capita and the average level of schooling are significantly lower than in urban areas. Pensions and other social benefits provided in urban areas are largely unavailable to the rural population.

Limits on integration with the rest of the economy did not prevent the rural sector from providing two key sources of China's development during much of the reform area. The first came from a major transformation in the policy environment in agriculture in the early 1980s. The tightly-controlled commune system of pre-reform times was replaced by a household based system in which individual farmers lease their land from the collectives, are largely autonomous in their production decisions, and bear the profits or losses from their operations. Market forces have largely replaced government plans and targets. And with the important exception of grains,[3] government intervention in the production, pricing, and marketing of agricultural products is now limited.

© OECD 2002

These policies have been instrumental in raising agricultural productivity and living standards during the reform era. The increase in agricultural productivity provided the first major impulse to the take-off in China's growth during the first half of the 1980s. However, the physical constraints on China's land and environmental resources make it difficult to increase productivity further within the existing pattern of production. Fertiliser use is already exceptionally high and the scope for increasing the use of pesticides is limited by their adverse environmental impacts. Water shortages and other environmental problems pose increasing barriers to higher agricultural productivity.

Fundamental improvements in agricultural productivity depend on substantial reallocation of resources away from land-intensive products toward labour-intensive products. However, the scope for reallocation is limited by certain government agricultural policies, the most of important of which is the grain procurement system. The policy has also had adverse consequences for macroeconomic performance in recent years: grain surpluses and falling market prices have depressed agricultural incomes and contributed to a marked slowdown in rural consumption growth.

The changing role of agriculture within the rural economy has provided a second major source of China's growth and development. In 1980, agriculture employed virtually the entire rural workforce and supplied nearly all of its income. However, rising productivity within agriculture was accompanied by the large-scale exit of workers from agriculture to industry.

In order to employ the workers coming from agriculture, local governments were encouraged to foster the growth of rural non-agricultural enterprises (REs), commonly known as TVEs.[4] These REs have been the main vehicle for absorbing this exit of workers from agriculture. REs are small and medium-size enterprises (SMEs) in rural areas that specialise in labour-intensive products, and along with foreign funded enterprises produce most of China's exports. Exemption from central planning restrictions, backing from local governments, business relations with state-owned enterprises (SOEs), greater exposure to market discipline compared to SOEs, and access to cheap rural labour, led REs to flourish beginning in the mid-1980s. They were the largest contributor to growth in aggregate GDP and employment from the mid-1980s through the early 1990s, and by 1996 employed 131 million workers, or 28 per cent of the rural workforce. The development of REs in turn has transformed rural income generation, with more than 40 per cent of rural incomes now coming from non-agricultural activities (Table 2). The overall effect has been to increase the interdependence between the rural and urban economies, even though the traditional administrative distinctions have largely remained.

The large-scale shift of workers from lower productivity occupations in agriculture to higher productivity jobs in industry has been an important engine of China's

© OECD 2002

Table 2. **Rural household incomes by source**
Net income *per capita*, per cent

	Year				
	1985	1990	1995	1998	1999
Total income (monetary and in-kind)	100	100	100	100	100
Of which: farming and related activities[2]	75	74	63	57	53
Memoranda:					
Total annual income in 1999 RMB[3]	1 311	1 370	1 718	2 132	2 210
Annual real growth rate, per cent[1]	..	0.9	4.6	7.5	3.7

1. Average growth rates for the periods between indicated years.
2. Including animal husbandry, forestry, fishing, hunting and gathering.
3. RMB amount deflated by the consumer price index.

Source: Figures are taken from Chapter 16, Table 16.4, which gives additional details. Data come from *China Statistical Yearbook* 2000, Tables 10-14 and 10-15. The data are derived from official household budget surveys using partly different definitions in urban and rural areas. Wages are assumed to be paid entirely in money.

growth, as it has been for other rapidly developing countries in the past. However, in China the bulk of the shift has taken place within the rural economy rather than through migration from rural to urban areas, due to government regulations that have impeded migration from rural to urban areas. These impediments, which amount to disincentives to migration rather than outright barriers, derive primarily from two sources. The first is related to the *hukou*, and has effectively denied services, other benefits, and most formal sector jobs in urban areas to rural migrants. The second impediment arises from the rural land tenure system, under which farmers who are absent for prolonged periods of time from their rural residences risk losing the land-use rights that are their primary old-age insurance.

Moreover, the shift of agricultural workers into REs has also been quite uneven. These industries have developed mostly in coastal provinces and have much less of a presence in the interior provinces, particularly those in the west. Even during the most dynamic phase, the growth of REs has not been sufficient to fully absorb the exit of workers from agriculture. The result has been the development of a substantial surplus of under-employed rural workers. A large portion of these workers – as many as 100 million – have become "floating" migrants who have taken up unregistered informal sector employment in urban areas.

The impetus to aggregate growth from REs has also waned in recent years. Since 1996, RE performance has deteriorated sharply, and employment has fallen by nearly 2.5 million. The slowdown in China's export growth after the 1997 Asian crisis can explain only a small part of this deterioration, which is rooted in fundamental structural problems. China's REs are suffering from financial problems and operating inefficiencies nearly as severe as those afflicting the SOE sector. The

© OECD 2002

exemption from central planning restrictions and sponsorship by local governments, which gave REs an advantage in the past, have become less important as constraints on SOEs have been relaxed. The disadvantages of REs, in terms of distance from infrastructure and other facilities that benefit businesses in urban areas and which limit the scale of operations REs can achieve, have become more prominent. The degree to which these disadvantages are offset by access to lower cost but also lower skilled labour is unclear.

China's further opening to international markets offers opportunities to revive the growth forces from the rural economy but does not ensure the opportunities will be exploited. China's undertakings in agriculture under the WTO include tariff reductions and higher import quotas, elimination of the privileged position of state-trading enterprises (STEs), and increased scope for private traders in the marketing of agricultural products. The opening to international markets implies a shift of resources away from land-intensive products, notably grains (except rice) and cotton, and an increase in resources in labour-intensive products such as vegetables and horticultural products. However, several policies not covered by China's WTO accession agreement, notably government control of grain procurement prices and distribution, will need to be changed if this reallocation is to occur to more than a limited degree.

Nor does opening appreciably alter the scale of the challenge of employing China's rural workers. Estimates suggest that, even with no further opening, nearly 70 million additional workers will exit agriculture between 2000 and 2010.[5] WTO itself is expected to add only 2 to 3 million further to this decline. The analysis in the chapter on rural industries indicates that, even under optimistic assumptions about how much their performance can be improved, REs are unlikely to be able to take up more than a fraction of the rural workers who will need to find jobs outside the agricultural sector. This further underscores the fact that the development of the rural economy is increasingly dependent on conditions and policies affecting the economy as a whole.

Structural impediments to further industry development[6]

Two related structural changes have provided much of the impetus to China's industrial development during the reform period. The first is the shift from a wholly state-owned industrial sector at the beginning of the reform period toward one increasingly dominated by "non-state" enterprises, starting with TVEs and other collectively owned businesses, followed by foreign-funded enterprises, and more recently by private domestic enterprises. Enterprises either wholly owned or controlled by government entities now account for less than 30 per cent of industrial output, although they still employ nearly half of the urban workforce in the formal sector.

© OECD 2002

This transformation of industry ownership contributed to growth in at least two ways. First, it fostered a shift of resources toward enterprises that have been more efficient and more effective in responding to changing market forces than most SOEs. The fact that non-state enterprises have faced harder budget constraints than many SOEs partly accounts for this superior performance.

Second, ownership transformation helped to spur growth by increasing competition. The entry of non-state enterprises engendered particularly fierce competition in export industries and industries supplying foreign goods, where the state has allowed relatively free access. Competition has been increased further by the curtailing of central planning mechanisms and freeing of prices: nearly 90 per cent of retail prices are now completely market determined, the main exceptions being energy and other utility prices. Increased competition has helped to raise the overall profit orientation of industry. The advance of competition has, however, been uneven. Protected industries reserved entirely or mainly for SOEs include major utilities such as electricity and petroleum/gas extraction, but also mineral extraction, steel and other metallurgical industries, automobile production, basic chemicals, and tobacco.

The second structural change is the progressive opening of the Chinese economy to foreign trade and investment. China's average tariff rate has fallen from above 40 per cent in the early 1990s to 15 per cent in 2001. Since 1979, China has received a cumulative total of US$ 350 billion in foreign direct investment (FDI) and in recent years, foreign investment has averaged 4-5 per cent of GDP (Table 3). The performance admittedly has been uneven: the bulk of foreign direct investment has come from Chinese Taipei, Hong Kong, China, and other Asian countries with large ethnic Chinese populations, while China has been less successful in attracting foreign direct investment from OECD countries.[7] Foreign direct investment has been largely concentrated in coastal provinces, mainly because most of the special economic zones (SEZ) granting preferences to foreign investment have been established in those regions.

The opening to international trade and investment has increased competition, spurred the growth of domestic labour-intensive industries, especially REs, and helped to develop China's exports. Foreign-invested enterprises (FIEs) in China have also been instrumental in developing China's export industries, particularly in recent years as foreign direct investment inflows have shifted toward capital- and technology-intensive export sectors. Foreign investment has also helped to raise industry productivity and to improve industry technology, know-how and the skills of workers.

As in agriculture, the dynamism to industry imparted by structural shifts seems to be weakening. Industry financial performance has deteriorated sharply since the early 1990s. Profits fell to nearly zero in 1998, with more than one-third of

© OECD 2002

Table 3. **Ratio of foreign direct investment inflows to China's GDP and gross capital formation**

	Total foreign direct investment inflows (US$ billion)	China's GDP (US$ billion)	Ratio of total foreign direct investment inflows to China's GDP (%)	China's domestic GCF[1] (US$ billion)	Ratio of total foreign direct investment inflows to China's domestic GCF[1] (%)
1983	0.916	300.375	0.31	101.483	0.90
1985	1.661	305.254	0.54	115.300	1.44
1990	3.487	387.723	0.90	134.705	2.59
1995	37.521	700.278	5.36	285.928	13.12
1996	41.725	816.490	5.11	323.148	12.91
1997	45.257	898.244	5.04	343.285	13.18
1998	45.463	958.990	4.74	356.964	12.74
1999	40.319	989.621	4.07	368.446	10.94

1. GCF refers to gross domestic capital formation.
Source: The Table is adapted from Chapter 10, Figure 10.2. Data come from various issues of the *China Statistical Yearbook*.

enterprises making losses, and despite noticeable improvement during 1999-2001, financial performance remains weak in many sectors. Growth in industry employment and capital spending has declined markedly. The deterioration has been pervasive and not simply confined to SOEs. The performance of collective enterprises has worsened nearly as much as that of SOEs; and the SME sector generally is in particularly dire straits.

The poor industry performance can be traced in part to the accumulation of policy burdens arising from the long-standing use of enterprises to accomplish social policy goals. These burdens, which amount to government resource extraction through regulation, include excess labour, high debt loads, and responsibilities for public pensions, housing, education, and other social benefits that in other countries are the responsibility of government or individuals. Policy burdens are heaviest on SOEs but they are also borne by REs. Authorities have made significant progress in recent years in reducing excess labour and excess capacity and in reducing debt burdens of larger SOEs. However less progress has been made in reducing other policy burdens, and there has been much less improvement for other SOEs or non-state enterprises.

The biggest problem impairing industry performance is widespread inefficiency in enterprise operations. Presently, much of industry operates with inadequate resources that are poorly managed by the firms that control them and which are misallocated across firms. In contrast to formerly centrally planned economies in Eastern Europe, China's industry is characterised by widespread sub-optimal scale in production facilities, fragmentation and duplication. There

© OECD 2002

are 200 separate producers of automobiles, most of which complete only a few thousand units per year. Much of the plant and equipment is outmoded. Economies of scope are also poorly exploited, as illustrated by the nearly 8 000 independent cement firms in China compared to 110 in the United States, 51 in Russia, 58 in Brazil, and 106 in India.

Inadequate technology and limited capacity to innovate are particular weaknesses of much of Chinese industry. Technology standards for a large portion of domestic firms are below international standards. China devotes proportionately fewer resources, and produces less scientific outputs such as patents, than OECD countries, as well as other large developing countries such as India. Industry also plays a relatively smaller role in technology development and innovation. Moreover, the technology transferred by foreign enterprises to Chinese firms seems to have been limited in both amount and scope.

These inefficiencies are attributable to a range of factors at the firm level, in the external environment, and in the relation between government and business. The poorly skilled and insufficiently profit-motivated management that characterises much of domestic business has neglected technology. Weak financial discipline, which has effectively presented firms and their government backers with a zero cost of capital, has been a major impetus to the development of unproductive and redundant capacity. The pre-reform policy of encouraging regional self-sufficiency together with low capital mobility has left a legacy of limited regional specialisation in production. The resulting inefficiencies have persisted and accumulated because key corrective market mechanisms have been severely impaired. Exit via bankruptcy and liquidation has been relatively rare, although it is becoming more common; and regional protectionism and other administrative barriers have severely restricted the scope for value-enhancing mergers and acquisitions (M&A). These factors have become a mutually reinforcing vicious circle (Figure 2). Government interference leads to poor SOE management and inefficient operations, which foster low profits and high debt; this in turn makes it more difficult to restructure to improve efficiency and prompts government interventions that spread the problem by extracting resources from stronger enterprises to prop up those that are failing.

Industry problems have become acute at a time when the traditional distinctions among ownership forms are becoming less and less meaningful in functional terms. Smaller SOEs and REs are blending into the broader universe of SMEs. Non-state enterprises are moving closer to enterprises formally recognised as private. The blurring of distinctions among ownership classes has not, however, appreciably levelled the playing field among enterprises even though it has modified the boundaries. The different ownership classes are still subject to distinct legal and regulatory frameworks. Differences in treatment – among smaller *versus* larger enterprises, among enterprises in competitive

© OECD 2002

Figure 2. **The vicious cycle of poor enterprise performance**

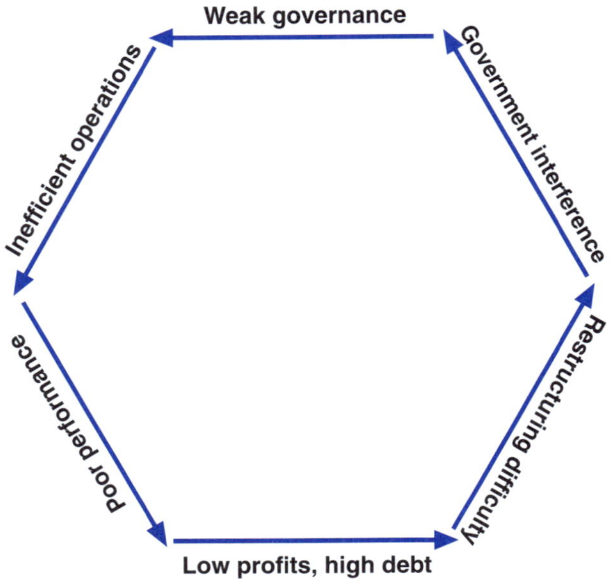

Source: OECD Secretariat.

versus sheltered sectors, and among enterprises that receive backing from central or local governments versus those that do not – remain and in some cases have increased.

The contrast in performance among industry segments has likewise become starker. Large SOEs remaining under government control receive preferential treatment from the government and are often sheltered from competition, but their performance is often lacklustre and their flexibility is constrained by government intervention in their management and by various policy burdens. A contrasting segment includes less favoured SOEs and collectives that have become highly competitive in national, and in some cases international, markets, in large part because they have been freer of government interference, more exposed to market discipline, and better managed as a result. Within this group are enterprises in consumer goods and other labour-intensive industries that have been tempered by fierce competition and have successfully integrated

© OECD 2002

into international production chains. Between these groups lie a large portion of (mainly) SMEs in poor financial condition and in dire need of restructuring, but whose ability to restructure is circumscribed by limited access to financing and other impediments.

China's further opening to international markets will force substantial adjustments in industry.[8] Studies indicate that production of textiles, particularly lower value-added segments, could more than double once the Multi-Fibre Agreement (MFA) is phased out in 2005. Other labour-intensive industries are expected to gain, although not as dramatically. Domestic firms in a number of capital or technology intensive industries are expected to lose ground, at least initially, to foreign competition. These include automobiles along with segments of the chemical and metallurgical industries. Foreign direct investment is also expected to rise substantially, by as much as two-fold annually by 2005 compared to the level that would otherwise prevail. Higher foreign direct investment will create jobs but will put competitive pressure on current domestic enterprises, even in sectors where China has a comparative advantage.

Trade and investment liberalisation is unlikely by itself, however, to restore dynamism to China's industry. To take full advantage of trade and investment liberalisation, the real economy will require extensive restructuring of firms, improvement in their governance and management, and reallocation of resources. The benefits of trade and investment liberalisation to particular industries will depend not only on their theoretical comparative advantage but also upon their ability to restructure and upgrade operations to meet the challenges of world markets that in important respects have become more difficult over time. For example, higher end segments of the textile industry will need to improve technology and quality if they are to keep up with competitors in other emerging Asian economies. Firms producing labour intensive products will need to integrate into international production chains if they are to be successful in export markets. Trade and investment liberalisation should help to improve some of the mechanisms needed to accomplish the necessary restructuring, by increasing competition, expanding opportunities for alliances between foreign and domestic firms, and spurring government officials to take measures to improve the business environment. However, key obstacles that now exist to improvement in industry performance, such as continued government interference in enterprise management, poor financial discipline, and restrictions on exit and other modalities for re-deploying resources, need to be addressed if the potential benefits of trade and investment liberalisation are to be realised. Furthermore, a more comprehensive and effectively enforced competition law will be needed to prevent incumbent firms and governments from erecting new protectionist barriers to subvert trade and investment liberalisation and the adjustments it will necessitate.

© OECD 2002

Figure 3. **Equity market capitalisation: ratio to GDP in selected countries, 2000**

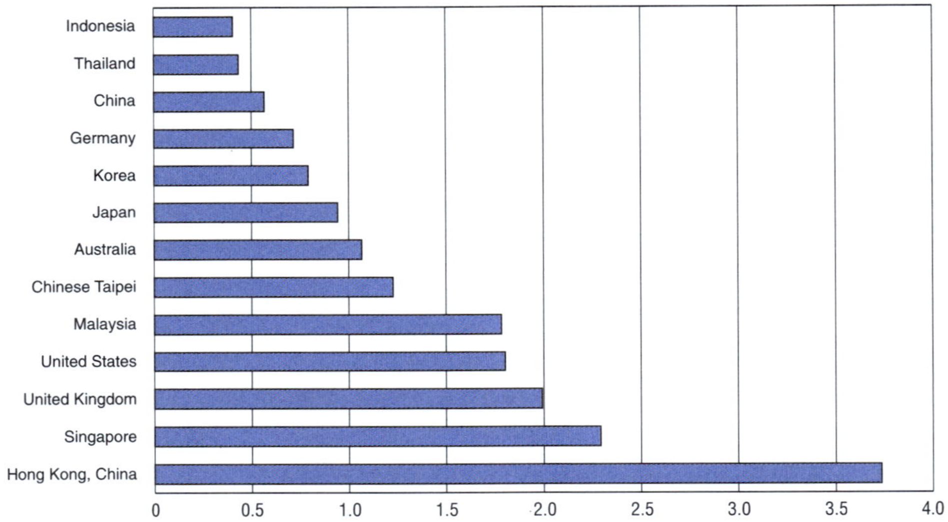

Note: Figure is from Chapter 15, Figure 15.1.
Source: International Federation of Stock Exchanges and OECD Secretariat Estimates.

Growing constraints from the financial system[9]

China's financial system has made important progress in recent years. The stock market has expanded impressively since its inception in the early 1990s, reaching a market capitalisation of more than 50 per cent of GDP by 2001(Figure 3). The past decade has also seen the creation of new nation-wide banks, significant expansion of the insurance sector, development of a domestic money market, and the more recent emergence of consumer and housing finance. The financial supervisory and regulatory structure has also been thoroughly reorganised and rationalised along lines consistent with international best practices.

Despite this progress, the financial system still performs inadequately in carrying out several of its basic functions in the economy. Although savings appear to be mobilised reasonably effectively,[10] credit is inefficiently allocated. SOEs receive the bulk of funds allocated by the formal financial system, while non-state enterprises receive a much lower share than warranted by their importance in the overall economy.[11] Non-commercial considerations, such as the need to sustain loss-making SOEs, continue to influence bank lending. These distortions, together

© OECD 2002

with the limited ability to vary interest rates to reflect risk, mean that the effective cost of credit varies widely among borrowers of comparable credit worthiness. There is limited diversity in financial outlets and capabilities. The interbank market and other available facilities provide only limited scope for transferring funds among financial institutions or regions. Insurance companies and other institutional investors are underdeveloped even compared with other emerging market economies such as India and Brazil. The government and other bond markets are small, fragmented, and illiquid, and the stock market, despite its rapid growth, is subject to limitations on access and trading that impair its effectiveness. Financial instruments to deal with liquidity fluctuations, manage risk, and provide for other specialised needs are limited.

The external discipline provided by the financial system has also been a major weakness. Years of government-mandated lending together with weak contract enforcement and bankruptcy regimes created a distorted credit culture in which banks have had limited incentives – and even less ability – to maintain strict lending standards and enforce loan contracts. Government mandates and weak lending standards created "soft budget constraints" for many enterprises that were a major factor in the over-investment that occurred during 1992-94, and whose legacy of excess and inefficient capacity now afflicts the Chinese economy. The overall weakness in discipline has been aggravated by its unevenness across enterprises. Due in part to the limited development of capital markets, but also to government intervention in enterprise operations, the financial system lacks means to support enterprise restructuring, re-deploy resources, and provide a market for corporate control.

These weaknesses in the financial system are partly a reflection of the fact that China is still a developing country. However they also reflect the fact that evolution of the financial system has lagged that of the real economy. Despite the substantial growth of the non-state sector in the real economy, the financial system remains virtually entirely state-owned (Table 4), with only a single privately owned domestic bank. The four major state-owned commercial banks (SOCBs) established in the early reform period to finance SOEs, and which are still heavily oriented toward this enterprise segment, dominate the financial system, accounting for nearly three-quarters of domestic lending. Credit facilities are segmented between the cities and rural areas. Operations of most commercial banks, with the exception of the SOCBs and 13 newer joint-stock banks, are restricted to their home city.

These structural features reflect the heavy past involvement of the government in lending decisions to support central planning mandates in the real economy and to use bank lending as a substitute for government spending to promote various non-commercial objectives. The latter practice was spurred in part by the steady decline in government tax revenues from the early 1980s through the

© OECD 2002

Table 4. **State ownership of banks**

	State owned or controlled banks: share of banking system capital	
	1998	1994
China	99	100
Other emerging economies:		
Hong Kong, China	0	0
India	82	87
Indonesia	85	48
Malaysia	7	9
Philippines	n.a.	19
Singapore	0	0
Thailand	29	7
Russia	36	n.a.
Argentina	30	36
Brazil	47	48
Chile	12	14
Mexico	28	0
Peru	0	3
South Africa	2	2
OECD *countries*:		
Australia	0	22
Canada	0[1]	n.a.
France	0[2]	n.a.
Germany	47	50
Italy	17[1]	n.a.
Japan	15	0
United Kingdom	0[1]	n.a.
United States	0	0
Czech Republic	19	20
Hungary	9[1]	81[3]
Poland	46	76

1. 1999.
2. The government has a controlling interest in several financial institutions that provide services similar to those of commercial banks.
3. 1990.

Sources: Chan-Lee, James with Sanghoon Ahn (2000), *Measuring the quality of financial systems in 29 market economies: an indicators approach with an extension to East Asia*, Asian Development Bank Institute, July; Barth, James R., Gerard Caprio Jr., and Ross Levine (2001), *The regulation and supervision of banks around the world: a new database*, World Bank, February; national sources and secretariat estimates.

mid-1990s (see Chapters 18 and 22 on tax policy and macroeconomic issues respectively). The resulting substitution of government mandates for sound credit standards is substantially responsible for the massive accumulation of non-

© OECD 2002

performing loans by banks and other financial institutions. Government involvement, and the perception that financial institutions will ultimately be backed by the government regardless of their performance, has also inhibited the development of a commercially oriented internal culture focused on the maintenance of sound lending standards and rigorous management of risks.

Beginning in the mid-1990s, the pace of financial reform has accelerated sharply in an effort to address the system's weaknesses. The banking law enacted in 1996 led to a significant tightening of bank lending standards by improving internal controls and strengthening accountability by holding bank loan officers and their management responsible for new problem loans. This step, together with the earlier establishment of three "policy banks", was intended to free commercial banks from government mandates. In 2000, authorities transferred RMB 1.3 trillion (about US$ 150 billion) of SOCB non-performing loans (NPLs), amounting to nearly 18 per cent of their total loans, to bank asset management companies (BAMCs). New joint-stock banks with nation-wide scope have been established since 1995 in order to create more diversity in the financial system. Authorities have also sought to reduce restrictions on the joint-stock banks to encourage their development and are planning to introduce governance reforms for SOCBs.

However, while important, these steps have not proved sufficient to remedy the weaknesses in financial system capabilities. Credit quality has improved but a large portion of SMEs now face a virtual credit crunch. While many of these enterprises are in poor financial condition, surveys suggest that lack of access to funding has become a key impediment to SME restructuring. Financial discipline has become if anything more uneven than before, as large SOEs with government backing continue to have good access to bank credit and have been the main beneficiaries of the additional financing provided by the stock market. Government intervention in lending decisions has been reduced but the continued provision of working capital loans to poorly performing SOEs suggests it has not disappeared. Furthermore, while the tightening of lending standards helps to contain new non-performing loans, it is unlikely to be sufficient to foster the managed risk-taking characteristic of commercially oriented financial institutions, and which will be increasingly needed in China to facilitate the adjustments to trade and investment liberalisation.

Financial weakness has made these problems all the more difficult to deal with. Despite the carve out of non-performing loans in 2000, the SOCBs along with many other financial institutions almost certainly would have negative capital if their loan portfolios were valued realistically. non-performing loans remaining with the SOCBs after the transfer of loans to BAMC were nearly 27 per cent of total loans in mid 2001 according to official figures, and would probably be higher if the international accounting and loan classification standards China is gradually introducing were fully applied. Joint stock banks also have high non-performing loans

© OECD 2002

and rural credit co-operatives are widely acknowledged to be in especially bad shape. Moreover, financial institutions have little cushion to write down non-performing loans: capital adequacy ratios are barely at the BIS minimum in the best cases and Ministry of Finance restrictions have left loan provisions at levels that are quite low by international standards. Bank profits have fallen steadily through the 1990s to very low levels that would probably be close to zero, or even negative, for SOCBs if international accounting standards were applied.

In a proximate sense, the ongoing problems of financial institutions reflect the poor condition of their enterprise customers. A severe vicious circle has developed (Figure 4). Poor enterprise performance contributes to bank non-performing loans and lowers bank profits by eliminating much of their core market. By themselves, financial institutions themselves cannot hope to restore their financial solvency unless and until enterprise performance improves substantially. But high non-performing loans make it difficult for banks to provide the funds for the enter-

Figure 4. **The vicious circles of bank and enterprise problems**

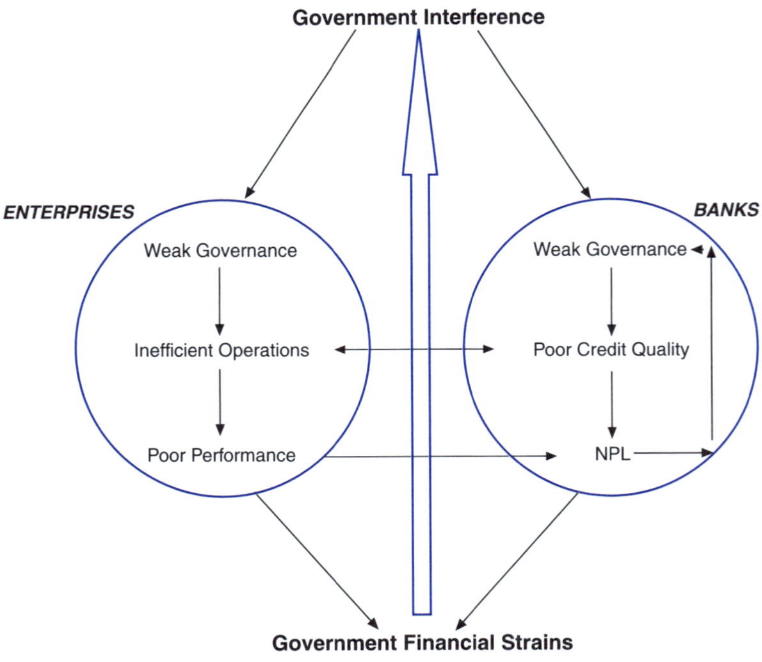

Source: OECD Secretariat.

© OECD 2002

prise restructuring needed to improve their performance. While common to countries in financial distress, this vicious circle is aggravated in China by behaviours derived from the traditional relations among financial institutions, SOEs, and the government that reforms have not yet decisively transformed. Limited government revenues to facilitate SOE restructuring and its consequences continue to require bank lending to sustain loss-making SOEs. This in turn weakens efforts to improve the internal credit culture and commercial orientation of the banks, while blunting incentives of SOEs to improve their own governance and management. The combination of financial weakness and inadequate governance of financial institutions and enterprises also creates risks that inhibit the development of healthy capital markets as alternative financial outlets.

As in other areas, trade and investment liberalisation offers opportunities but cannot itself guarantee that domestic problems will be appreciably reduced, and it presents some risks if these domestic reforms are not effective. Trade and investment liberalisation in principle allows much greater scope for foreign banks, insurance companies and securities firms to participate in the domestic market. Concerns within China that domestic banks will lose a substantial market share to foreign banks appear to be overstated, however. Foreign banks are likely to be very selective in their activities and to largely avoid lending to domestic enterprises until their performance improves substantially.[12] As argued in the chapter on the banking sector, the development of China's domestic banks depends on the success of reforms to improve their capabilities and governance *and* to facilitate restructuring of their enterprise customers. Given success in these areas, foreign entry into banking and other financial services should help to develop the financial system, and ultimately benefit Chinese firms that succeed in improving their capacities to operate effectively. Trade and investment liberalisation is also likely to increase foreign investment in China's capital markets. This is likely to help develop these markets over the long-term, but it may put near-term pressures on Chinese equity markets, where domestic shares appear overvalued compared to those on international markets. Opening of the capital markets to foreign participation on any sizeable scale implies liberalisation of the capital control regime – which will require substantial improvement in financial discipline and supervision if risks to financial stability are to be contained.

Emerging weaknesses in macroeconomic performance[13]

China's macroeconomic performance has been enviable in many respects. Impressive growth in real GDP has been accompanied by even more rapid growth in foreign trade and investment that have made China one of the more open of the world's largest economies.[14] The external balances have remained healthy. China has undergone several episodes of overheating and inflation during the reform

© OECD 2002

period, but has avoided the prolonged bouts of very high inflation suffered by many other developing countries.

In recent years, however, several signs of a weakening in China's macroeconomic performance have emerged. The first is the slowdown in real growth noted earlier. Real GDP growth since 1996 has averaged slightly above 8 per cent, nearly 2 percentage points below the pace of the prior fifteen years. Fiscal stimulus, which contributed nearly 1 percentage point to growth during 1998-2000, prevented an even greater slowdown. Employment growth has fallen even more sharply (Figure 5), to below the rate needed to absorb new entrants into the labour force plus those laid off from SOEs and other activities. The result has been a marked rise in urban unemployment – which by some estimates is over 10 per cent – and a further increase in under-employed rural workers.

The slowdown is not fundamentally cyclical. China was hit only moderately by the 1997 Asian crisis and growth has remained low by past standards even as Asian countries recovered. Nor does the slowdown seem to reflect the natural decline in potential growth that occurs as countries run out of opportunities to transfer labour from low productivity to higher productivity occupations and to absorb readily available technology and know-how from abroad. The labour surpluses and widespread inefficiencies in industry suggest that these processes

Figure 5. **Aggregate employment growth**

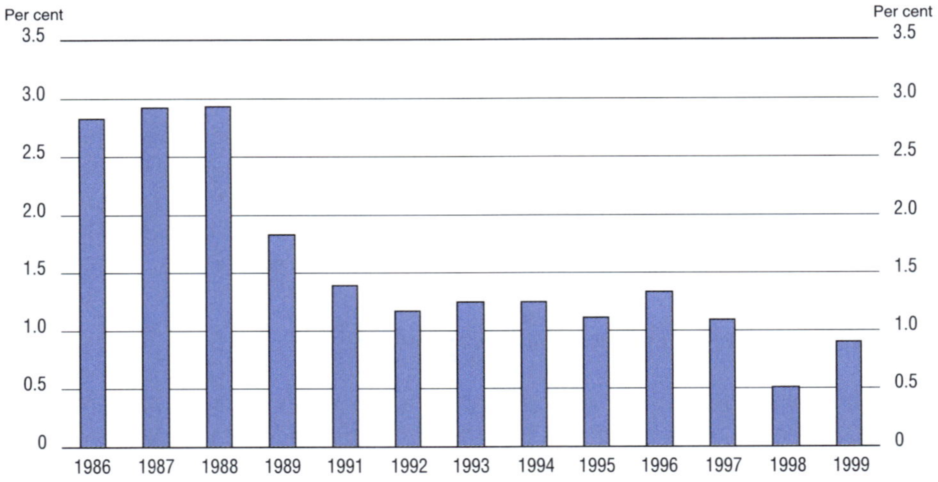

Source: China Statistical Yearbook, 2000.

© OECD 2002

have been slowed by structural distortions but are not exhausted. Rather the growth slowdown is more plausibly viewed as the result of the drag on aggregate demand engendered by the problems of banks and enterprises, together with structural problems in the rural economy.

The slowdown in real growth also poses challenges to authorities as they seek to foster the adjustments needed to alleviate the structural problems. Adequate growth is needed to generate the demand, profits, and government revenues required to finance industry upgrading, facilitate reallocation of resources among sectors, and support workers displaced by the transition. Achieving full employment of the labour force is likely to require an extended period of growth above China's potential rate at some future point.

Efforts to support growth through macroeconomic stimulus have underscored the limits on monetary and fiscal policy instruments. As has happened in OECD countries during periods of banking stress, expansionary monetary policy has had only a limited impact because of the credit crunch resulting from banks' reluctance to risk incurring new problem loans. Although the central bank interest rate has been lowered progressively, to below 1 per cent currently, bank-lending rates have been allowed to fall by less in order to avoid further aggravating the weak profitability of the banks.

As a result, fiscal policy had had to supply most of the macroeconomic stimulus. Official figures suggest that China's fiscal position is healthy and that there is ample scope for fiscal expansion. While the general government deficit rose to nearly 3 per cent of GDP in 2000, domestic and foreign government debt together still amount to only about 32 per cent of GDP.[15] However, this picture is misleading because it is widely acknowledged that the government will need to take on debt obligations not yet explicitly recognised. The main obligation, the funds needed to restore solvency to financial system, could more than double the government debt ratio initially.[16]

China's debt-carrying capacity is probably less than its GDP might suggest because government revenues are relatively low. Tax revenues fell steadily relative to GDP between 1980 and 1996 and, although they have recovered somewhat, are still less than 15 per cent of GDP. General government revenues, including "extra-budget" fees collected by local governments and contributions to social insurance funds, are about 21 per cent of GDP, a relatively low level compared to OECD countries as well as a number of emerging market economies (Table 5).

The relative scarcity of government revenues has had broader consequences. Government spending on education, research and development, and other social purposes have been low by international standards. The imposition of policy burdens on enterprises and the use of bank lending as a substitute for explicit

© OECD 2002

Table 5. **Government on-budget revenues as share of GDP**
Figures for 1999

	Percentage share
China	20.4
OECD average	37.8
United States	31.0
European Union	45.0
Japan	37.6
Other emerging market economies	
Brazil	31.7
India	18.8
Indonesia	17.3
Russia	29.8

Source: OECD Secretariat compilations and estimates based on national sources. Date include payments to social insurance funds.

government spending is due at least partially to the scarcity of government revenues. Limited revenues at the local government level, due in part to distortions in the present fiscal federalism arrangements, have encouraged the widespread imposition of unsanctioned *ad hoc* charges and other forms of resource extraction on enterprises and rural residents. These distortions account for a striking paradox in China's fiscal system. Government financial resources to facilitate economic reforms and meet other key social needs are limited; yet the burden of government resource extraction is heavy for most segments of the real economy – including those that appear to receive preferential treatment in the formal tax system.

The macroeconomic consequences of China's WTO entry are difficult to predict.[17] Much will depend on the success of the economy in making the necessary microeconomic adjustments and on the degree to which economic reforms allow the potentially large dynamic gains from trade and investment liberalisation to be realised over the long term. Adjustment to trade and investment liberalisation will stimulate some sectors but engender deflationary pressures from sectors that lose ground. Macroeconomic policy is likely to have to deal with a shifting balance between these positive and negative forces over time. Recent commentaries point to the possibility that the current exchange rate parity may need to be changed at some point as trade and investment liberalisation proceeds – but they differ as to the direction. These considerations suggest that greater flexibility will be needed in macroeconomic demand management instruments and in the exchange rate regime and capital control regimes.

© OECD 2002

Growing imbalances in regional development[18]

China's growth during the 1990s has been accompanied by growing inequality among its regions. Incomes and living standards have risen in nearly all areas, but growth has been most rapid in the coastal provinces, followed by provinces in the central region, and least rapid in the western regions (Table 6). Geographic disparities in income have been rising steadily since the late 1980s.

Table 6. ***Per capita* GDP and real GDP growth by province**

	Per capita GDP RMB/capita		Rank in the year		Change of rank	Growth rate of GDP	
	1980	1999	1980	1999	1980-99	1980-90	1990-00
Eastern							
Beijing	1 582	19 803	2	2	0	8.8	10.9
Tianjin	1 392	15 932	3	3	0	7.3	11.5
Hebei	427	6 913	12	11	–1	9.2	12.8
Liaoning	768	9 958	4	8	4	8.4	9.4
Shanghai	2 738	30 805	1	1	0	7.4	12.2
Zhejiang	468	11 981	9	4	–5	11.1	15.0
Jiangsu	544	10 699	6	7	1	11.6	14.0
Fujian	343	10 969	20	6	–11	11.4	15.4
Shandong	405	8 648	14	9	–5	10.1	19.6
Guangdong	473	11 739	8	5	–3	12.8	14.6
Guangxi	281	4 264	26	25	–1	7.2	11.6
Hainan	278*	6 227	27	15	–12	11.7	12.5
Central							
Shanxi	437	5 117	10	18	8	8.7	9.4
Inner Mongolia	345	5 400	19	16	–3	10.6	9.8
Jilin	384*	6 302	17	14	–3	9.5	10.4
Heilongjiang	685	7 660	5	10	5	6.9	8.4
Anhui	285	4 710	25	21	–4	9.9	12.2
Jiangxi	342	4 673	21	23	2	8.8	11.7
Henan	317	4 899	23	19	–4	9.6	11.5
Hubei	428	6 511	11	13	2	9.2	11.9
Hunan	365	5 227	18	17	–1	7.8	10.5
Western							
Chongqing	–	4 852		20	–		
Sichuan	315	4 356	24	26	2	8.1	10.0
Guizhou	219	2 463	30	29	–1	9.5	8.7
Yunnan	367	4 444	28	25	–3	11.8	9.3
Tibet	259		29		–	6.4	9.2
Shaanxi	335	4 107	22	27	5	10.0	9.1
Gansu	388	3 595	16	28	12	8.8	9.4
Qinghai	475	4 707	7	22	15	7.1	8.2
Ningxia	409	4 477	13	24	11	9.7	8.5
Xinjiang	405	6 653	15	12	–3	11.1	9.7

Source: *China Statistical Yearbook*, 2000.

© OECD 2002

The divergences in growth rates and increasing gaps in living standards among China's regions, and between urban and rural areas, are fundamentally reflections of their poor integration. Transportation and communication infrastructure within China's interior provinces, and that linking the interior with the coast, is generally much less developed than in the coastal provinces. Segmentation has been accentuated by differences in market rules and conditions across regions, and in the way government policies are applied. The scope for non-state enterprises has been considerably less in interior provinces than on the coast, and the heritage of SOE dominance and past central planning is greater. Capital mobility has been limited, due in part to the limited outlets for transferring savings among regions and to protectionist barriers to business establishment across regional jurisdictions. Largely as a result of the pre-reform policy of regional self-sufficiency together with limited capital mobility, there is relatively little regional differentiation in industrial production structures, suggesting that regional comparative advantages are not adequately exploited. There are several competition bodies and conditions governing business establishment often differ among provinces. Until recently, interior provinces were given much less freedom to offer preferential treatment to attract foreign direct investment compared to the coastal provinces, and in some cases have been further disadvantaged by the closure of their resource sectors to foreign participation. As discussed in Chapter 9, the relatively inefficient distribution system has increased costs of marketing products nationwide and has fostered regional segmentation in some product markets.

Government policy to favour the development of coastal provinces has increased their integration with the international economy to a degree that in some respects exceeds their integration with the rest of the domestic economy. While the policy is intended to catalyse the development of the economy as a whole, the spillover benefits are limited by the poor integration of the coast with the interior. The focus in the current five-year plan is to continue to rely on the coast to lead China's growth while improving infrastructure in the interior, mainly western, provinces and allowing their governments to offer financial and other preferences to attract foreign direct investment and domestic capital. These efforts are intended to provide a foundation for the much longer-term goal of reducing disparities in growth and, eventually, in living standards. Apart from these measures, explicit regional policy has largely been left to provincial authorities. Financial and other key reform policies at the national level have few explicit regional dimensions.

China's approach to regional policy presents a marked contrast to the experience of the European Union. From the beginning, EU policy emphasised the integration of its internal markets in parallel with liberalisation of its international trade and investment regimes. The example of the United States, which has enjoyed a high degree of internal integration for many years, has been a motivating

© OECD 2002

factor behind this emphasis. Internal integration in the EU has been an explicitly broad based effort to allow free movement of goods, services, capital, persons, and businesses. In order to create comparable conditions for business operations across member countries, the European Commission is assigned responsibility under the Treaty of Rome for enforcing competition law, and has undertaken complementary initiatives toward greater harmonisation of tax and other policies affecting the business environment. The motivation for this move to a "single market" has been that internal integration can have benefits at least comparable to those from external integration, and indeed is necessary to fully realise the benefits of external trade and investment liberalisation.

Trade and investment liberalisation is widely expected to increase pressures for divergences among China's regions – despite the initiatives being taken under the western economic development programme. Although governments in interior provinces are making strong efforts to attract foreign investment, most foreign direct investment is expected to go to coastal provinces. The labour-intensive industries that will benefit most are also concentrated in coastal provinces. Their proximity to international markets and their infrastructure also favour coastal producers of vegetables and other labour-intensive agricultural products. Without further policy efforts, income inequalities among regions are expected to grow, and could even accelerate with trade and investment liberalisation.

Improving the utilisation of China's resources

China's economy is clearly operating below its productive potential. Human, capital, land, and other resources are under-employed, misallocated among economic sectors, and inefficiently used. Achieving better resource utilisation is the most basic challenge China faces in seeking to meet its development objectives. As discussed in this section, better integration among the various segments China's economy is likely to be essential if resource utilisation is to be improved. Many of the priorities and suggested steps outlined below, and summarised at the end in Box 2, will need to be supported by complementary policies to improve market framework conditions and to strengthen the capacity of the government to support economic development.

Raising labour utilisation[19]

The task of achieving full employment of China's workforce is daunting. Rough projections indicate that China's aggregate labour force will increase by more than 70 million over the next decade. To absorb these new entrants along with the millions of workers expected to leave agriculture, while making progress toward reducing the number of under-employed, will require substantially more rapid employment growth in industry and services than has been attained in recent years.

© OECD 2002

Given the widespread structural distortions in the economy, macroeconomic policy, although it has an important complementary role to play, can do little in the medium-term if inflation is to be contained. Instead, achieving better labour utilisation is fundamentally a structural challenge. Labour market reforms are a necessary pre-condition to achieve this goal, but broader reforms discussed later will also be required.

The key priority for improving the capacity of labour markets is "... *to overcome an inherited pattern of labour market segmentation and establish a national labour market*".[20] This is necessary because, whatever purposes they may have served in the past, impediments to rural-urban migration and other impediments to mobility have become major obstacles to absorption of excess labour and improvement in labour productivity. Removal of labour mobility constraints is necessary not only to allow workers to find jobs but also to reduce other distortions. In particular, access to a wider array of jobs should improve incentives for rural workers to increase their human capital. Increasing the supply of labour to urban areas should stimulate development of urban businesses. Integrated labour markets should foster business location to areas offering the greatest comparative advantages in terms of access to resources, suppliers, and markets.

An essential step toward creating a national labour market is to begin to progressively phase out the constraints on migration to urban areas and other barriers to the recruitment of non-local workers by urban enterprises. Reform of the *hukou* is necessary to reduce these impediments and has recently been endorsed in principle by the Chinese authorities. Several local experiments with its relaxation are underway. The step has broader implications that condition its timing: in particular, the phase-out might begin with medium-sized cities followed later by larger cities. Furthermore, to genuinely improve labour mobility and integration, *hukou* relaxation needs to be accompanied by reforms of the rural land tenure system if rural migrants are not to face a prohibitively large loss of their land assets. Reform of land tenure, whose terms vary widely, is also necessary to ensure that migration incentives are comparable across regions.

While a key step, elimination of *hukou*-related constraints on rural-urban migration and land tenure reform are only first steps. Other complementary measures need to be taken, beginning in the near-term and extending over a longer period, to improve labour market flexibility and to ensure that improved mobility results in greater and higher productivity employment in the economy as a whole. Local preferences and other measures within and between urban areas that inhibit migrants from seeking education or finding jobs in the formal sector also need to be eliminated in a timely fashion. Development of the unemployment insurance system to replace the transition arrangements being used to help laid-off SOE workers should help to improve incentives for efficient job-search. OECD experience suggests that unemployment insurance reforms can be reinforced

© OECD 2002

through the establishment of a modern employment service that works with businesses to improve collection and dissemination of information – but which does not seek to interfere with hiring decisions.

Over a longer period, development of SMEs in or near cities in interior provinces needs to be fostered along with the expansion of existing cities and creation of new cities in areas where they are economically viable. This will be necessary to ensure that rural migrants from these provinces can find jobs without a mass exodus to coastal cities, and the attendant excessive congestion and negative externalities such an exodus would likely create.

Improved labour market performance also depends importantly on broader reforms to social programmes. Achieving higher educational standards in order to improve human capital is a key priority in this regard, particularly in rural areas where education expenditures and attainment lag those in urban areas considerably. A longer-term goal suggested by OECD experience would be to raise the average duration of formal education from the current 9-10 years to 12 years, and to increase the portion of students that complete the first level of higher education (*i.e.* 16 years) to 25 per cent.

Better integration of the markets also depends on reforms to increase the coverage and portability of pensions and other social benefits. While achievement of these objectives is necessarily a longer-term goal, more attention needs to be paid in the medium-term to relieving distortions that arise from the unevenness in financing burdens for the government-run first tier of the pension system. These distortions are greatest between rural and urban enterprises, and between the informal and formal sectors within the urban sector, and are due to the currently limited and uneven coverage of pension benefits. These differences have worsened as required contribution rates for enterprises subject to the formal pension system have increased. A first step would be to reduce disparities that now exist among urban areas, possibly by pooling financing of the first tier of the pension system at the provincial government level, rather than at the municipal level as is now the case. Over the longer-term, coverage will need to be extended to rural workers and those now in the informal sector in cities, but with flexibility to allow some local variations in contribution and benefit rates.

Making better use of land and environmental resources[21]

The key to improving productivity in the agriculture sector is to "... foster cropping patterns and other agricultural decisions based on emerging market opportunities and regional comparative advantage, rather than on the traditional yardstick of increasing grain output in all areas at any cost".[22] As indicated in the last section, land and other resources now devoted to grain production need to be shifted toward more labour-intensive crops if China is to be able to exploit its

© OECD 2002

comparative advantage under trade and investment liberalisation. To achieve this goal, the current system of government control over grain procurement prices and the related interventions should be phased out as import restrictions are eliminated. This is likely to be needed in any case to contain fiscal burdens on the government.

This step will have greater benefits if accompanied by other complementary policies. These include development of information systems concerning output and input prices and improved marketing channels. Improvement in product standards and quality that are consistent with international norms is particularly important if China is to fully benefit from the opening of foreign markets to agricultural products in which it has a comparative advantage. Infrastructure investment to better link farmers with their markets is also important, particularly in interior provinces. As the experience of European transition economies has underscored, restructuring in agriculture, and in the rural sector as a whole, requires adequate financing. Improvement in the functioning of the rural credit co-operative network and its better integration with the rest of the financial system is basic in this respect. Development of other micro-financing and informal credit channels, provided they can be structured and supervised to prevent abuse, could be particularly effective in the small-scale and low-income farming environment in China.

Reallocation of agricultural production will help to promote an important environmental goal, which is the severe shortage of water and degradation of water quality in Northern China. Water use has expanded sharply over the past twenty years due to increasing use of irrigated land and to growing demands from rural industries and urban centres. Reduction of land-intensive grain crops should release water resources to accommodate urbanisation or other uses. The recent adoption of a more market-oriented water pricing policy, based in part on actual supply costs, should also help to promote more efficient use of water resources.

China's other major environmental problems are extensive air and water pollution. Nearly one-third of the country suffers from acid rain, urban air pollution is quite severe in larger cities, and there are growing pressures on solid waste disposal facilities. These problems can be traced to a variety of factors, including low energy efficiency and the reliance on soft coal in energy generation, the increased use of fertilisers in agriculture, urbanisation, and the explosion in the automobile population in urban areas. The trend away from heavy toward lighter and generally less polluting industries has moderated these forces somewhat, but not enough to prevent a continuing deterioration in environmental quality.

China's government has been making strong efforts to alleviate pollution problems. Environmental standards have been tightened substantially and the authorities have been encouraging more efficient energy use and a shift away from coal toward oil and other less polluting sources. Local governments have been

© OECD 2002

shutting down enterprises that are in violation of pollution standards. These and other steps have substantially established the legal and regulatory framework needed to achieve China's environmental goals. However, as in many other areas, the effectiveness of the framework is limited by implementation problems.

Trade and investment liberalisation will potentially contribute to alleviating China's environmental problems by spurring the shift toward more labour-intensive industries. However the extent to which the environmental benefits are realised depends on reducing three main barriers that are limiting the effectiveness of current policy. The first is better enforcement of environmental regulations, particularly of national standards that are often evaded or ignored at the local level. The power of courts to interpret environmental laws and to adjudicate disputes between legal and regulatory provisions needs to be strengthened. Second, subsidies, price distortions, and other adverse incentives that encourage pollution and inefficient energy use need to be phased out. And third, there needs to be better co-ordination among government agencies to develop a more comprehensive environmental strategy and to redress the significant gaps and "responsibility vacuums" in environmental policy formulation and enforcement at all levels.

Bolstering the capacity of the business sector to productively employ resources[23]

Labour market reforms can improve the conditions under which labour is supplied but improvement in the capacity of the business sector to productively employ both labour and capital is equally critical. An important longer-term goal is to foster the development of China's service sectors, particularly labour-intensive services, but the pace at which this occurs will depend on further increases in urbanisation. The more immediate priority is to restructure China's industrial enterprises through consolidation and reorganisation to achieve a more efficient structure of industry as a whole. Technology also needs to be upgraded and industry's capacity to innovate and to absorb new technology strengthened.

China's government has long been heavily and directly involved in industry restructuring. Since the 1980s, authorities have sought to develop large enterprises and enterprise groups as "national champions" to compete in international markets with multinationals from more advanced economies – although these efforts have met with little success. More recently, the government has intervened extensively and directly to reduce excess labour and other policy burdens of SOEs, to lower surplus capacity, and to manage SOE restructuring. While these efforts have had important benefits, they have also distorted the restructuring process, for example by requiring stronger enterprises to merge with weaker firms. Much of the government involvement reflects its continued intervention in SOE management. Government efforts have also been focused on large SOEs destined to remain under state control.

© OECD 2002

A key message of the study is that *market mechanisms need to be strengthened so that they play the dominant role in China's business restructuring*. Fundamental improvement in the performance of China's industries will involve extensive reallocation of resources, and changes in ownership and control extending across thousands of enterprises in both the state and non-state sectors. SMEs are critical to this effort and their importance will further increase as the economy shifts toward more labour-intensive activities. These changes will need to come about primarily from market driven processes in which individual enterprises reorganise to maximise the long-term value of their operations. While trade and investment liberalisation offers opportunities to large Chinese enterprises, success in international markets has come to depend less on the scale of a multinational's operations than on the sophistication of its management and the effectiveness of its governance –qualities over which government can have little direct control. Given these conditions, government policies to promote restructuring need to focus on establishing conditions that support market restructuring processes, such as improving competition and clarifying property rights, while limiting direct interventions to matters, such as the disposition of SOE assets, where market processes alone are insufficient to accomplish the task.

The most pressing need is to remove obstacles that now exist to market driven business restructuring. Two sets of policies are most essential to accomplish this objective. The first is financial system reform, as discussed further in the next sub-section. It will not be possible to shift resources toward enterprises that can use them most efficiently unless credit allocation is much more firmly based on strict commercial criteria than is now the case. For this to happen, banks and other financial institutions will need to have greater capacity and better incentives to lend to productive outlets. Financial markets need to be more flexible and open if they are to facilitate transfers of ownership and create a market for corporate control. OECD experience also offers lessons for improving access to external financing for creditworthy SMEs, as part of broader efforts to develop this key enterprise segment.

The second key step is to end government interventions that constrain enterprises' ability to reorganise, distort their incentives to do so, and which block their exit when needed. SOEs particularly need to be given autonomy to choose the partners and terms for mergers and acquisitions based on their long-term economic value, without being burdened by non-commercial requirements imposed by government authorities. SOEs also need to have clearer claims and control over their assets if they are to be able to restructure their operations in a productive manner. Regional barriers to capital mobility and to cross-provincial business location also need to be curtailed. Policies that have the effect of creating cartels or price floors (including rules that define pricing below industry average cost as "predatory") should be avoided wherever possible since these tend to limit

© OECD 2002

incentives for restructuring and to slow exit. Equally important are reforms to facilitate and accelerate exit, since large numbers of China's present enterprises are not competitively viable and will need to leave the market if industry is to become more efficient.

While such measures are essential first steps, their ultimate payoff depends on reforms in other areas. These include measures to eliminate external conditions that would tend to distort restructuring decisions, such as unequal social benefit burdens and incentives that encourage regional protectionism. Equally important are reforms to corporate governance and other framework conditions discussed in the next section that are needed to ensure that enterprises have the capacity and incentives to exploit value-enhancing restructuring opportunities. In light of experience and the more demanding international market environment, authorities might also review the current policy of developing national champions and consider narrowing its focus to areas where China's current advantages give it a better chance of success than in the past.

The technology challenges facing Chinese industry further underscore the importance of strengthening market forces while improving the quality of government intervention. Meeting these challenges involves more than simply making more technology available to the market. Other key objectives are to foster the improvement of capacities at the firm level to innovate and to use and absorb technology; to improve technology diffusion; and to enhance the technological pay-off from foreign direct investment. Explicit technology policies cannot achieve these objectives by themselves without broader reforms. In particular, bolstering firm abilities and incentives to keep up with market technology standards requires improvements in management and governance, competition, and other framework conditions necessary to ensure that firms are adequately profit-oriented. Equally important are reforms to improve protection for intellectual property rights to encourage technology sharing and the development of venture capital facilities. Further opening of knowledge-based service sectors to foreign participation would also help to foster technology transfer from abroad.

The government has an important role to play in improving China's technological capabilities but there needs to be a change in emphasis. The government is likely to have to supply much of the resources to bring funding for basic science up to levels more comparable to international norms. OECD experience suggests that China's government can contribute to technology diffusion by providing support to regional university and other research centres, for example. There is also a need to embed government technology policies in a broader framework that exploits complementary relations with other industrial policies. This is likely to require greater co-ordination between the Ministry of Science and Technology, which has been largely responsible for technology policy, and other Ministries responsible for programmes concerning financing for SMEs and other industrial policies.

© OECD 2002

Box 1. Improving technological capabilities – Some potential lessons from OECD experience

OECD experience offers some lessons for fostering the development, diffusion, and absorption of technology. It shows that successful new technology-based firms – which are responsible for an increasing share of innovations – require not only superior governance and management capabilities but also an enabling infrastructure of business services.

The experience of OECD countries indicates that effective implementation of technology diffusion programmes requires organisational improvements and strategic changes in firms, the building of interactive relations between different players, exploitation of existing resources and a local presence. To accelerate technology diffusion, OECD governments are focusing on addressing market and systemic failures through four types of operational strategies:

- *Supply-driven initiatives* that transfer technologies developed under government sponsorship to the private sector. An example is the Canadian Space Agency's Space Station Program, which involves competitive bidding of private firms for contracts to develop and commercialise dual-use space technologies.
- *Demand-driven programmes* seek to diagnose and enhance the technological absorptive capacity of firms. The Manufacturing Extension Partnership in the United States assists smaller manufacturers to implement appropriate technologies and improve their business practices.
- *Network-building initiatives* develop bridging institutions and inter-firm partnerships to facilitate information flows. Innovation Centres in the Netherlands strengthen both vertical and horizontal network links at the regional level.
- *Infrastructure-building programmes* upgrade the technology diffusion infrastructure at the national level. Korea adopted various schemes of spreading new technology and promoting network links as part of the country's developmental strategy.

Absorption of technology is a long-term process in which acquiring firms need to develop long-term partnerships and trust with technology providers. Case studies of the electronic and semiconductor industries in Korea and Chinese Taipei suggest that it is important for domestic firms to engage in progressively more advanced forms of technology transfer with foreign partners over time (for example, from subcontracting, to technology licensing to OEM, to ODM, to joint product R&D and strategic alliances).

Despite its impressive performance, there is significant room to improve China's foreign direct investment performance in both quantitative and qualitative terms. The strengthening of intellectual property rights protection under China's accession agreement should help to attract more foreign direct investment from developed country businesses, which have sometimes been reluctant to

© OECD 2002

invest in the domestic market out of concern that their advanced technologies and production techniques will be inadequately protected. Given the worldwide trend toward the use of M&A in cross-border investment, establishment of market based mechanisms for domestic M&A would also help to attract investment from more advanced economies. Adoption and effective enforcement of a comprehensive competition law, and reduction in administrative and other barriers beyond those required by the WTO, would encourage more foreign investment aimed at the domestic market. Further opening of protected industries, for example by allowing more foreign participation in extractive activities, would also help to attract foreign direct investment as well as increase efficiency.

Other measures could help to improve the pay-off to the domestic economy from foreign investment. Improved competition and better enforcement of contracts would encourage more local sourcing of inputs, such as packaging materials, used by resident foreign enterprises. Reduction of government interference in the operations of domestic enterprises could help to foster more fruitful partnerships with foreign firms possessing advanced technology.

Improving the effectiveness of the financial system[24]

Improvement of the capabilities of the financial system to promote efficient resource utilisation is fundamental to the restructuring of industry, achieving better integration among regions, bolstering macroeconomic performance, and allowing China to open its financial markets to the world without undue risk to financial stability. As noted earlier, despite the important steps taken over the past five years, the fundamental capabilities and incentives of the financial system to allocate credit efficiently remain impaired.

As discussed in the previous section, the problems of the financial system are closely linked to those of the real economy and to the shortage of resources effectively available to the government. As emphasised in the chapter on the banking sector, China's banks are unlikely to become fully healthy and effective until the performances of their enterprise customers improve substantially. Nevertheless, international experience strongly indicates that timely and decisive reforms of the financial system are essential to break through the vicious circle China now faces. Three key objectives need to be achieved if the financial system is to become an effective support, rather than obstacle, to the broader reform process.

The first and most pressing objective *is to restore capital adequacy to financial institutions within the near-term*, through direct government financial support as needed. International experience suggests there are a range of specific modalities that could be used to accomplish this objective, but that three important principles need to be observed if the benefits are to be realised.

© OECD 2002

- First, the rehabilitation needs to be thorough, comprising measures to deal with non-performing loans (through removal from banks' balance sheets of non-performing loans that cannot be dealt with out of provisions or through write-downs) and increases in capital, to at least the BIS minimum initially.
- Second, the clean up should complete the financial rehabilitation of SOCBs, and address the non-performing loans of other commercial banks and credit co-operatives that are also in distress.
- And third, the clean up and its aftermath should also involve strict conditions on the financial institutions, under which management is held accountable for, and given the requisite autonomy to improve, future performance. For example, authorisation for banks to enter new lines of business could be made conditional on their maintenance of adequate capital and adherence to prudential standards.

While a necessary precondition, balance sheet clean up cannot itself guarantee sustained improvement in the effectiveness of the financial system. Perhaps the most basic lesson from other countries' experiences with financial distress is that clean up needs to be accompanied by stringent measures to correct the conditions that led to the stress. In China's context, measures to establish and strengthen the governance of financial institutions as commercial entities and further improve their internal systems for credit assessment and management of risk are essential, along with the strengthening of the independence and capabilities of bank supervisors. These are particularly necessary given the inevitable difficulty of ensuring that government-owned financial institutions, particularly large ones, are truly commercially oriented,

Nevertheless, international experience strongly suggests that breaking the vicious circle China is now in requires early intervention to restore financial system solvency as other measures to improve conditions in the real economy that require more time are undertaken. Inadequately capitalised financial institutions tend to have weak incentives to maintain sound lending standards or manage risk.[25] Indeed, financial weakness can spur perverse incentives to hide loan problems or to take excessive risks ("gamble for redemption"). In China's case, stronger balance sheets are necessary to allow other reforms to improve the fundamental health of financial institutions to proceed. These include the ability of banks to restructure to meet increased foreign competition and to access external funds to bolster their capital. Moreover, given their low profitability, China's financial institutions are unlikely to be able to achieve capital adequacy out of their own resources within a reasonable time. In fact, balance sheet clean up is probably key to their longer-term ability to improve their profitability.

While the current rapid pace of loan growth might suggest that banks could "outgrow" their high non-performing loans rates given sufficient time and continued

© OECD 2002

rapid growth in the real economy, such a strategy carries important risks. It would leave banks in even worse shape if loan or deposit growth were to slow. It could also pose a difficult dilemma between improvement in banking system conditions and fostering the growth of alternative financial outlets which might divert business from banks. As the experience of other countries, most recently Japan, has underscored, relying on real sector recovery to restore the health of financial institutions is more likely to impede real recovery, allow financial problems to get worse, and increase the ultimate cost of their resolution.

There has been concern that a government sponsored clean up will undermine financial institutions' incentives to sustain a strong credit culture. Against this must be set the fact that only SOCBs benefited from the first non-performing loans programme, and the widespread perception within and outside China that the government will always back the solvency of the SOCBs in order to prevent a financial crisis. Delay in restoring solvency is more likely to increase and prolong expectations of multiple and open-ended bailouts. A second concern is whether China's government can afford the cost of a thorough financial system clean up, given the limits on its fiscal resources. The cost is likely to be high, on the order of those facing other Asian countries that experienced severe banking problems in the aftermath of the 1997 crisis.[26] However, as argued in the last section of this summary, the cost should be affordable provided that government revenues continue to rise relative to GDP, social benefit programmes are established on a sustainable basis, and further non-performing loans are kept to minimal levels. China does not now face an intractable dilemma between cleaning up the financial system and maintaining the sustainability of its fiscal accounts. But further delay, since the ultimate costs are likely to rise, increases the risk that such a dilemma will develop in the future.

Restoration of solvency will also help to promote the second, if longer-term, objective, *to create a more diverse and balanced system in which financial outlets other than SOCBs have a much greater role*. The SOCB orientation toward SOEs is likely to continue, as they become "lead banks" for the large firms that will remain under state control. This, together with their size and potential ability to tap domestic and international financial markets, gives them a strong comparative advantage in serving multinational and other larger enterprises. The other commercial banks and credit cooperatives probably have stronger comparative advantages and incentives to lend to SMEs, but their ability to expand their market share is circumscribed by regulatory and other limits on their access to funding. Accordingly, relaxation of policies that restrict the ability of joint stock and other smaller institutions to expand, as part of broader efforts to create a more level playing field among commercial banks, are necessary first steps toward greater diversity in the financial system. A more active longer-term policy to restructure the SOCBs along regional or functional lines would also help to promote greater diversity and to increase competition.

© OECD 2002

Greater diversity would also help to improve the commercial orientation of the financial system as a whole. Although strong efforts are being made to develop a more commercially oriented credit culture in the SOCBs, the task is inevitably difficult given the traditional role of these banks in central planning, their continued strong ties to the government, and, not least, their "too big to fail" status. The joint-stock banks enjoy more autonomy from government mandates, are generally better managed and more commercially oriented. Increasing the importance of these banks would help to make the overall banking system more responsive to market forces.

The third key objective to improve financial system capabilities *is to foster the development of China's capital markets.* The government bond market needs to be able to absorb the large increase in public debt that is likely to occur in the next several years. Capital markets are also necessary to allow enterprises to achieve a better debt and capital structure and to provide the instruments for retirement savings that will be needed as the second and third tiers of the pension system develop. However, China's capital markets are not yet capable of adequately carrying out these functions. Most listed companies are SOEs and only about one-third of their shares are actively tradable. The market has been prone to manipulation and overvaluation. The bond, as well as money, markets are behind the stock market in their development and lack liquidity and breadth. As argued in Chapter 15, the markets as a whole will need further strengthening to accommodate new financial instruments, greater foreign participation and increased exposure to international financial markets at acceptable risk.

As in other areas, the priorities for improving the capital markets start with several near-term steps to remove obstacles to their effective functioning and development. These steps have been endorsed by the authorities (or at least raised by senior officials), but in some cases their implementation has been delayed.

- The first is to increase the share of SOE equity that can be traded within the three year time-period authorities have specified, following a pre-announced timetable.
- The second is to open stock market listing to all firms, including collectives and private firms, based on their ability to meet the supervisory requirements – thereby ending the preferential treatment large SOEs still receive in this area. This, together with the first step, is basic to improving the discipline offered by the stock market and to creating a market for corporate control.
- The third step is to integrate the equity markets by eliminating the distinction between ("A") shares that can be held by Chinese citizens and the ("B") shares that can be held by foreigners within the near term. This step does not depend upon achievement of capital account convertibility, but it will need to be carefully timed to avoid disruptions arising from the now considerable differences in share valuation across the segmented markets.

© OECD 2002

These near-term steps should open the way for, but also need to be reinforced by, other policies to promote the development of the capital markets over the medium and longer-term. These include policies to improve corporate governance and to allow foreign financial institutions to enter the capital markets, and implementation within the medium-term of official plans to improve the government bond market. Frameworks for mortgage bond and mortgage-backed bond markets will need to be established in order to facilitate the increased demand for real-estate credit as housing reforms proceed.

Achieving better integration among China's regions[27]

Better integration among China's regions is not simply important on equity grounds. Lack of integration is becoming an impediment to other development goals and is likely to become a greater obstacle over time if not addressed. Without greater integration, coastal and a few interior cities are likely to bear the brunt of the migration of workers who will need to find jobs in cities. The resulting pressures on urban land, the environment, and other resources could lead to sharply diminishing returns from agglomeration, and thereby degrade the advantages that have given these urban areas their vitality. Greater integration is needed to make full use of China's land and agricultural resources – which cannot be transferred to the coast. Continued segmentation among regions limits the productivity gains from regional specialisation and restricts the ability of enterprises to achieve adequate economies of scale and scope.

To achieve better integration, China needs a much broader and comprehensive regional development strategy focused on the creation of national markets for products and productive factors. This implies a shift in emphasis, away from the granting of selective exemptions from government regulations and tax preferences, in favour of measures to allow greater scope for national market forces and to improve the ability and incentives of local governments to respond to those forces. OECD experience underscores several pitfalls in regional development strategies that are potentially relevant to China, including:

- over-reliance on government interventions to develop specific areas or sectors ("growth poles") to catalyse regional development, a strategy which tends to be quite expensive and has proved to not be very successful;
- the launching of major infrastructure projects without taking realistic account of regional demand; and
- maintenance of direct assistance to declining sectors in order to protect local economic activities.

In addition to infrastructure development, a comprehensive regional development strategy for China involves three basic objectives. The first is to ensure that common framework conditions for competition, property rights, business

© OECD 2002

establishment, and taxation apply to all regions and localities. As the experience of the EU suggests, this is likely to require a sustained and broad initiative from the central government. The principle that sub-national governments may not impose barriers to domestic trade, which is contained in current law but lacks enforcement provisions, needs to be strengthened. This might be accomplished (as in the European Union and Russia) partly through the application of national competition law provisions.

The second objective is to improve the mobility of capital among regions. Development of national capital markets and improvement in the commercial orientation of financial institutions are the ultimate keys to promoting a more efficient geographic allocation of capital over the longer-term. In the near-term, administrative burdens on local business need to be reduced and transparency in regulations increased if provincial governments in the interior are to be competitive in attracting foreign direct investment as well as domestic capital. Reduction in administrative barriers and local protectionism that impede cross-border business establishment and mergers and acquisitions is also important. In the medium term, further development and liberalisation of the money markets and expansion in the geographic scope for city bank operations in the interior would facilitate the ability to transfer savings among regions. Opening of protected resource sectors to foreign investment would also help to attract foreign direct investment to resource-rich central and western provinces.

Regional integration also depends on a third objective, reform of central-local government fiscal relations. The current system contributes to the unevenness in tax burdens among regions. As discussed in the last section of this synthesis, the allocation of government revenues and division of responsibilities for spending need to be realigned among government levels in accordance with need rather than the economically arbitrary administrative criteria. China needs not only to raise the total amount spent nationally on education but to give equal priority to increasing resources for education in rural areas, particularly those in the interior, where standards are now low but the potential payoff in terms of improved human capital is relatively high.

Realisation of the benefits of greater integration also depends on promoting greater balance in urbanisation by fostering market-driven creation and development of new cities in interior provinces. City building along with the exit of workers from agriculture will help to equalise strains on urban resources and provide an impetus to regional growth as agglomeration economies are exploited. Expansion of existing medium-sized cities by accretion of bordering rural townships that are already experiencing rapid growth of new enterprises should also help to invigorate growth. Creation of new cities, however, is a complex process in which the most productive role of government is to foster conditions conducive to their formation. These include access to financing and sufficient flexibility in labour

© OECD 2002

Box 2. Key priorities for improving resource utilisation

Problem	Priority objectives	Some suggested steps
Labour market segmentation is preventing full employment of human resources	Create a national labour market by removing impediments to labour mobility	*a)* Beginning in the near term, progressively phase out *hukou* related restrictions on migration and reform rural land tenure *b)* Continue to develop the unemployment insurance system and reduce disparities in social benefit burdens over time
Government policies impede a shift away from land-intensive toward labour-intensive crops	Foster cropping patterns in line with market forces and regional comparative advantage	In the near term, phase out controls on grain procurement, prices and distribution
Environmental problems impair efficient resource allocation	Improve enforcement and achieve better co-ordination of environmental policies among government agencies	Strengthen the powers of courts to interpret and enforce environmental laws and regulations; eliminate distortions that encourage pollution and inefficient energy use
Business sector restructuring is hampered by lack of market mechanisms	Foster market-based mechanisms as the primary vehicle for restructuring	*a)* In the near term, remove government imposed obstacles to enterprise restructuring *b)* Develop capital markets over the longer term
Technology is sub-standard and capabilities for innovation, diffusion, and absorption are weak	Develop a comprehensive framework to foster technology capabilities of enterprises	*c)* Improve protection for intellectual property rights; increase government resources devoted to basic R&D
Credit allocation is inefficient, financial discipline is weak, and financial facilities to support business sector restructuring are limited	*a)* Restore financial system solvency *b)* Improve diversity in financial institutions and develop money and capital markets	*a)* Restore capital adequacy to financial institutions in the near term subject to strict performance requirements. *b)* Remove regulatory barriers impeding the functioning and development of money and capital markets as soon as possible *c)* Over a longer period, foster a greater role for joint-stock and other smaller commercial banks; foster development of capital markets, in part by liberalising access of foreigners to the capital markets

© OECD 2002

Box 2. **Key priorities for improving resource utilisation** (*cont.*)

Problem	Priority objectives	Some suggested steps
Regional fragmentation is becoming an obstacle to broader development needs	Develop a comprehensive regional development strategy, focused on the creation of more uniform framework conditions and improving internal capital mobility	*a)* In the near term, eliminate administrative and other regional protectionist barriers *b)* Reform central-local government fiscal relations within the medium-term *c)* Promote development of national money and capital markets

markets to attract essential labour skills, along with sufficient autonomy for regional and city planning authorities to formulate and implement development strategies based on local resources and comparative advantage.

Strengthening the institutional frameworks for market functioning

The success of the steps to break down barriers to resource reallocation and to ensure that resources are efficiently used in the future depends critically upon governance, property rights, competition, and other frameworks essential to effective market functioning. Considerable effort has been made over the past several years to strengthen several of these frameworks, but their impact has been blunted by the more limited progress made in complementary areas. Fundamental ambiguities in the property rights framework have not been resolved; market discipline is still inadequate; and while organisational structures and many of the basic laws have been established, their effectiveness has been limited by inadequate enforcement. This section outlines the priorities for strengthening the frameworks; these are summarised in Box 3 at the end.

Strengthening enterprise governance[28]

Establishing governance structures so that enterprises behave as autonomous profit-seeking commercial entities has been a key goal of China's economic reforms since the early 1990s.[29] The difficulties facing China in accomplishing this task are hardly unique. OECD countries have experimented for several decades with various modalities for ensuring that publicly-owned companies

© OECD 2002

perform adequately – but with only limited success. The difficulties in China are likely to be even greater, given the close ties between the government and SOEs.

Since 1999, corporate governance reform focused on SOEs has become a key priority in China. The strategy has sought to create governance structures patterned on best practices derived from OECD-country experience.[30] One component of the strategy is the conversion ("corporatisation") of SOEs into legally independent joint-stock companies and the establishment of boards of directors and supervisors together with laws defining their responsibilities and those of managers. With this, the authorities have sought to curtail direct government intervention in enterprise management by creating separate organs to manage state-owned assets. The second component, which has been given increasing emphasis, is to list corporatised SOEs and diversify their ownership in order to provide further discipline on the boards and managers. Nearly half of SOEs have so far been corporatised. Authorities plan to corporatise the SOCBs within the next several years.

The tangible results of the governance reforms have fallen short of expectations, however. Actual corporate governance practices deviate considerably from OECD standards, and surveys indicate that China is still seen as comparing unfavourably to its Asian competitors in this regard.[31] Weaknesses in the structures themselves are one reason for the limited success of the reforms. The boards of directors and supervisors mandated by corporatisation do not yet have sufficiently distinct identities within the enterprise and their independence is limited. Top managers continue to be appointed by local authorities or political officials. The boards tend to function more as an extension of management than as its monitor, and are effectively bypassed in exercising genuine oversight. The autonomy of managers is weakened by their dependence on government or political authorities for their position, their low salaries, and their lack of a direct stake in the firm's profit performance.

Two related steps needed to improve the functioning of the existing corporate governance framework are to *strengthen the independence and powers of boards of directors and to foster greater accountability and professionalism among managers*. Greater use of qualified independent directors, including outside directors, should be part of this effort. With this, the scope for political participation in enterprise governance should be limited to advice and consultation. These steps would help to lay the foundation for development of a market for managers, which is now lacking, and for the more widespread adoption of performance-based compensation.

The greater obstacles and necessary solutions to the present weaknesses in corporate governance lie outside the corporate governance structures themselves. Much of the difficulty in creating SOEs that are autonomous, profit-oriented, and accountable to their state owners can be traced to the ambiguities in the property

© OECD 2002

rights framework discussed further below. Partly as a result, SOEs have gained only limited autonomy as the result of corporatisation, and have continued to be subject to government restrictions on their ability to lay off workers, dispose of assets, and engage in mergers and acquisitions.

As in other countries, stronger market discipline is critical in establishing a firm and lasting foundation for effective corporate governance. In China, competition is often limited in sectors in which the current listed SOEs are concentrated. Apart from the continued weakness in discipline from financial institutions, limited access to the market and the withholding of the majority of listed SOE shares from trading effectively prevent the stock market from carrying out the disciplining role it has been assigned in the overall corporate governance reform strategy. The impact of ownership diversification has so far been blunted by the fact that nearly all of the minority shareholders are other public entities, whose own profit-orientation is often weak.[32] Strengthening external disciplines is particularly important because once the basic legal structures are established, their functioning depends most critically on market incentives for enterprises to maintain effective governance.[33]

Finally, corporate governance issues in China do not simply involve SOEs. Collective enterprises have multiple owners and stakeholders and their internal control, allocation of residual claims, and ties to local governments are also ambiguous and of limited transparency. Many collectives seem to be evolving into forms equivalent to joint-stock companies but without being required to adopt the governance structures of the latter. The need to establish a good credit standing and business reputation should create incentives for larger collectives to adopt governance norms more in line with those required of corporate firms. The degree to which this will be true for other collectives is less clear.

Reforming property rights and insolvency mechanisms

Property rights and their embodiment in contracts have been one of the major gaps in China's frameworks for market functioning. An essential step toward remedying this gap was taken in 1999 with the enactment of a Unified Contract Law to replace the formerly scattered collection of laws, by-laws, and regulations based on numerous and not always consistent legislative provisions. The new law creates clearer and more even rules of the game for contractual transactions among businesses of all types and establishes a national framework to which local authorities are subject. The law also reduces the scope for regulatory restrictions on contract provisions that are not sanctioned by other legislation.

The key remaining objective is to develop a coherent framework clarifying property rights and ensuring their equal application to all economic segments. Property rights remain highly ambiguous due to the unresolved status of state

© OECD 2002

assets and the relation between public and non-public ownership. Different sets of rules apply to private, collective, and state-owned property. SOEs cannot freely dispose of their land or of rights to its use.

Lack of clarity about the effective owners of SOEs is a major obstacle to their restructuring and improvement in their governance. SOEs are effectively owned by a collection of ministries and agencies at all government levels with unclear and often conflicting claims that are not adequately defined by existing law or regulations. This creates a situation that has been characterised as "agents without owners",[34] in which multiple owners have limited incentives to monitor the enterprises or to hold their managers and boards accountable. It also produces conflicts that slow and distort business restructuring and exit.[35]

Ambiguous property rights are also impeding restructuring in other parts of the real economy. Apart from the potential barrier to labour mobility posed by the rural property rights regime, the uncertain status of state assets poses obstacles to the development of private enterprises. Private enterprises are unlikely to realise their full potential until the rules for acquiring state assets are better defined.

There is thus a pressing need to develop a coherent framework and supporting laws clarifying rights to property and to ensure their equal application to all segments of the economy. Explicit protections for private property, and better definition of the rights of the enterprise as a legal entity *vis-à-vis* holding groups, regulatory agencies, and political bodies, are key elements of this framework.

Ambiguous property rights are also an impediment to China's insolvency mechanisms. Although bankruptcies and liquidations have increased markedly in recent years, they have occurred mainly among smaller firms and those in the private sector. Passage of the reformed comprehensive bankruptcy law that was first drafted in 1994 will be an important step toward establishing uniform rules applying to state and non-state enterprises and in defining the rights of debtors, creditors and shareholders. But further efforts are likely to be needed to improve the independence of bankruptcy courts and the professional skill of judges so that they can more effectively implement the legislation.

More also needs to be done to clarify the rules if insolvency mechanisms are to be able to accommodate the large-scale re-deployment of assets from nonviable enterprises that will be needed in coming years. Presently, exit is often blocked by legal and administrative barriers to disposal of claims of banks, bank asset management companies, social benefit funds, and agencies responsible for supporting displaced workers. The government agencies that are ultimately responsible for these bodies need to be held liable for these claims so that they do not prevent the liquidation of insolvent firms.

© OECD 2002

Improving the competition framework[36]

By some standard indicators, China's product markets appear to be reasonably competitive: market concentration at the national level is relatively low; and there has been substantial entry of new firms. Economic rivalry is fierce in many sectors. These measures are deceptive, however, because the limits to competition in China are manifest in other ways. Government restrictions are more prominent as barriers to competition. Limited transport facilities, local protectionism, and other barriers to geographic integration allow enterprises to exercise monopoly power in local markets to a degree that is not apparent in national concentration ratios. Moreover, as noted earlier, competition is uneven across sectors.

The main weaknesses in the competitive environment in China can be listed as follows.

- As has happened in other countries, established enterprises and local governments often seek to prevent entry by newcomers and thereby extract monopoly rents. Product market competition is limited in some cases by overt barriers, by distortions in the tax code and distribution system, and, probably most importantly, by locally imposed restrictions on outsider's ability to establish or acquire a local business.[37]
- The different legal and regulatory frameworks applying to state-owned, collective, private and foreign enterprises, along with complex and opaque requirements for business establishment and business scope, often limit competition. Examples include the high minimum capital required of private limited companies and their need to undergo an elaborate regulatory approval process to make even modest changes in their lines of business.[38]
- While prices are reasonably free to vary for most products and markets, they continue to be restricted in some, notably energy and tobacco. The temporary price floors imposed in industries with excess capacity also limit competition as well as impede exit.
- A substantial number of key sectors are wholly or mainly reserved to SOEs, including not only natural monopolies but, as noted earlier, automobile and steel production. Authorities plan to reduce the role of SOEs to "strategic sectors" but have not specified what those sectors will be.

The present competition law framework rests on the 1993 Unfair Competition Law and the 1999 Price Law, together with various specific regulations and decrees banning certain regional protectionist practices. These laws are enforced by the State Administration for Industry and Commerce (SAIC) and the State Development Planning Commission (SDPC). Together these laws outlaw some overt anticompetitive practices, such as price fixing, and prohibit unauthorised actions by local government agencies or officials that prevent competition. However these

© OECD 2002

laws do not constitute a comprehensive legal framework for competition. In particular, existing Chinese law does not clearly prohibit other practices, such as monopoly abuses, cartels, or restrictive distribution arrangements, that effectively prevent entry and restrict competition. Current prohibitions on anti-competitive practices by government agencies lack sanctions and have had little if any practical effect.

Given this situation, the key objective is to establish a national competition framework to ensure that laws and regulations support rather than interfere with market competition. Adoption of such a framework is particularly important since incentives to engage in anti-competitive practices are likely to increase with trade and investment liberalisation. An essential first step is to enact and implement a comprehensive competition law along the lines of that now being drafted by the State Economic and Trade Commission (SETC) and SAIC. This law should include effective sanctions against the maintenance of "administrative monopolies" by government agencies. As in OECD countries, China's government could usefully apply competition principles to identify existing and proposed laws and regulations that interfere with competition, with a view to eliminating those that are otherwise unwarranted. Special scrutiny should be given to laws that restrict entry based on the legal form or ownership of an enterprise. Competition policy principles should also be incorporated in the design of natural monopoly regulation.

Beyond these measures, steps need to be taken to reduce the incentives for anti-competitive behaviour, particularly that fostered by government entities. In this respect, reforms to social security, the financial system, and other conditions that encourage government entities to extract resources through anti-competitive behaviour are ultimately important to ensure a competitive environment.

Developing financial regulatory and supervisory capabilities[39]

The financial regulatory and supervisory (FRS) framework is key to the success of the steps discussed earlier to improve the capabilities of the financial system and to allow its further development without creating unacceptable risks to financial stability. China's financial regulatory and supervisory authorities face especially great challenges given the adverse incentives inherent in extensive state ownership of financial institutions.

Important steps have been taken since the mid-1990s to provide a modern institutional base for financial regulation/supervision comparable to that of OECD countries. In 1999 the People's Bank of China (PBC) was reorganised into nine regional branches in order to reduce local government interference in its operations and to provide a platform for more effective bank supervision. The PBC now has responsibility for all depository financial institutions, including the rural credit co-operatives. The previously fragmented responsibility for regulation and supervision of the stock exchanges, bond markets, and securities and investment

© OECD 2002

companies has been consolidated in the China Securities Regulatory Commission (CSRC), while responsibility for insurance companies has been lodged with the China Insurance Regulatory Commission (CIRC).

The key objective now is to strengthen the autonomy of financial supervisory authorities and to endow them with the necessary physical and human resources to accomplish their tasks. China's financial regulators face a particularly daunting task in maintaining prudential standards in state-owned financial institutions subject to other, sometimes conflicting, government mandates. As the essential starting point, supervisors need to have the authority and independence to exercise surveillance over supervised institutions solely in the interest of prudential soundness and in a way that is not constrained by other government objectives. Supervisors need to be able to require prompt corrective action by institutions subject to their jurisdiction when problems are found. While their authority has been strengthened in recent years, supervisory authorities still lack full control over some basic prudential standards, such as the power to impose realistic norms for bank provisioning and loan write-offs.[40] Financial supervisors will also have to continue to acquire the necessary physical and human capital to accomplish their tasks. Adaptation of internationally accepted supervisory norms and practices to Chinese circumstances is an important means to these ends – and one which will also provide a foundation for the ultimate opening of the financial system to international markets.

Supervisory structures and responsibilities also need to be further refined to keep up with the development of financial markets. The concentration of authority over capital markets in the CSRC and expansion of its institutional capacity have been essential steps toward ensuring effective oversight of the markets. However, the authority of the CSRC to investigate abuses and order remedies needs to be further strengthened, and accounting, disclosure, and audit standards should be aligned more closely with international practices. Newer financial vehicles, notably investment funds that take money from the public, need to be brought within a formal regulatory framework, preferably one based on models provided by major financial markets outside of China. The CSRC and supervisory authorities responsible for the insurance and pension fund sectors need to co-ordinate their efforts to ensure a level playing field for institutional investors.

Ultimately, the effectiveness of financial supervision in China, as elsewhere, rests on its success in ensuring that market participants have adequate internal incentives and capabilities to maintain prudential standards. Supervision needs to progressively increase the responsibility of market participants for in-house compliance with prudential standards, risk management, and adherence to industry standards. Effective corporate governance of all financial market actors is crucial to these goals. To this end, efforts to strengthen shareholder rights and to raise standards of corporate governance are an essential element of the supervisory process.

© OECD 2002

Improved transparency in the operations of all enterprises is essential for effective regulatory oversight and effective monitoring by investors and stakeholders. Several steps now underway should help greatly to improve transparency once they are completed. These include the implementation of new accounting standards for financial institutions that are more in line with international norms; and the extension to all non-financial enterprises of the modernised accounting standards that have been required of listed SOEs. Transparency needs to be accompanied by improved disclosure and measures to ensure the accuracy of the information reported. To this end, enterprises need to be further encouraged to bring in independent outside auditors to assist in preparing their annual reports. This should be facilitated by the increased scope foreign auditing firms are scheduled to receive with trade and investment liberalisation. Supervisory authorities, together with the relevant professional associations, need to make further efforts to increase the independence of auditing firms and their compliance with regulatory standards.

Improving the enforcement capacity of the judicial system

Weak enforcement of improved legal and regulatory frameworks has been a recurrent theme of China's economic reforms, ranging from enforcement of contracts, commercial codes, competition law, and environmental codes. The Chinese authorities are committed under their WTO agreements to improve judicial enforcement of contracts and other business codes, including those governing intellectual property and counterfeiting.

However, there has been little fundamental change in the judicial mechanisms for enforcement. Neither the independence of the courts nor their jurisdiction is adequately established. Although the Chinese constitution states that judicial proceedings are to be free of interference from other government and political entities, judges, courts, and other judicial organs remain under their supervision and dependent on them for funding. The legal obligations of other government entities to enforce or obey court decisions are not adequately established, and court decisions are often ignored as a result. The relations among courts are also unclear, which makes it difficult to reconcile conflicting rulings in different jurisdictions or to build a body of case law. Enforcement is further hampered by the limited experience of China's courts (which traditionally have been devoted to criminal matters) with civil law proceedings, and the limited training of judges and other judicial personnel.

To improve enforcement the key objective is *to strengthen the independence and clarify the jurisdiction of courts, particularly with respect to government bodies.* The Supreme People's Court has developed a plan for independent funding of the judiciary to curtail its dependence on local governments. For this to be effective, however, the process of appointing judges will need to be made more professional and less subject to political influence.

© OECD 2002

Box 3. Key priorities for improving frameworks for effective market functioning

Problem	Priority objectives	Some suggested steps
Corporate governance reforms have had limited success	Address remaining weaknesses in governance structures while clarifying property rights and strengthening market incentives	*a*) In the near-term, improve independence and accountability of managers and boards of directors *b*) Remove restrictions on trading of SOE shares as soon as possible and take other steps over the longer-term to improve financial market discipline
Ambiguous property rights hamper corporate governance and mechanisms for business sector restructuring	Develop a coherent framework and supporting laws ensuring that property rights are well defined and apply equally to all economic segments	In the near term, clarify and strengthen SOE rights to property and other assets; clarify rules governing use of and acquisition of state assets by non-state entities
Bankruptcy and other insolvency mechanisms are too weak to allow resources to be re-deployed from firms that are not competitively viable	Establish a more uniform framework for insolvency and strengthen the autonomy and enforcement powers of bankruptcy courts	In the near term, enact a comprehensive bankruptcy law with uniform rules and clear rights of debtors, creditors, and shareholders; clarify responsibility for debt of failing enterprises to banks and social benefit funds so that they do not block exit
Competition is uneven across sectors; anti-competitive practices and in some cases legal/regulatory frameworks impede entry or limit competition among incumbents	Develop a comprehensive framework for fostering competition nationwide with clear definition of the responsibilities of government agencies	*a*) In the near term, enact a comprehensive competition law; and establish a clear code of conduct sanctioning anti-competitive practices by government entities *b*) Except for natural monopolies, open sectors now reserved for SOEs to other enterprises
Weak financial discipline encourages misallocation of resources, weakens incentives of enterprises to operate efficiently, and poses risks to financial stability	Strengthen the independence and capabilities of financial regulators/supervisors; improve the ability and incentives of financial institutions and markets to provide discipline	*a*) In the near term, restore solvency to financial institutions while continuing to improve their accountability for maintaining sound prudential standards *b*) Move rapidly to strengthen enforcement powers of financial supervisors *c*) Improve transparency and remove restrictions on financial markets that inhibit discipline
Laws and regulations are poorly and unevenly enforced	Strengthen the independence of the judiciary and clarify its jurisdiction	*a*) In the near term, reduce the judiciary's financial dependence on government and political authorities and strengthen the jurisdiction of courts over government agencies

© OECD 2002

Improving the government's capabilities to support economic development

The need to periodically redirect the role played by government as the economy develops is not unique to China. OECD countries have gone through a comparable process during the post-war period, in building, restoring, and maintaining sound public finances, in seeking to develop tax structures that impose as little distortion as possible on the real economy and in undertaking regulatory reforms to improve market functioning. As discussed further below and summarised in Box 4, improvement in the ability of China's government to foster a successful adjustment to trade and investment liberalisation and to promote its longer-term development rests on the achievement of three key goals. The most immediate is to bolster public finances to establish a sustainable fiscal position in which adequate revenues are raised to meet the development needs of the economy. Reform of central-local government fiscal relations is an important element of this effort. The second goal is to strengthen and increase the flexibility of the policy instruments needed to maintain macroeconomic stability in the face of the diverse shocks the economy is likely to experience in coming years. And the third goal is to establish a comprehensive framework for regulatory policy to promote effective market functioning.

Bolstering public finances[41]

The strains on China's public finances are manifest in the under-funding of research and development, education, and other areas important to the economy's development, the difficulty of finding adequate government revenues to facilitate restructuring of SOEs and to expand social benefits, as well as the proliferation of *ad hoc* fees and charges imposed by local governments. As noted earlier, demands on public finances will grow substantially even in the medium term. The scale of these demands has led at least one prominent scholar to warn that China's fiscal position may be heading for a crisis.[42] However a crisis should be avoidable provided that three conditions are met.

The first is an *increase in tax revenues in relation to* GDP *to levels needed to accommodate increases in spending for development needs.* Tax revenues have been rising relative to GDP in recent years (Table 7) and there is significant scope within the current tax structure for them to increase further. The potential yield from improved collection of the value-added tax (VAT),[43] which accounts for more than one-third of total tax revenue, is especially great. Taxes on services and personal income are likely to increase relative to GDP as services and urban household incomes continue to grow rapidly, and could be increased further if collection were improved. There is also scope for enterprise income taxes to rise relative to GDP provided that restructuring succeeds in raising their profitability. Rough calculations suggest that

© OECD 2002

Table 7. **Annual growth in tax revenue, 1994-99**

	Growth (%)	Share of total 1999
Total	15.8	100
Value-added taxes	11.0	36.3
Business taxes	20.0	15.6
Consumption taxes	11.0	7.7
Tariff revenue	15.5	5.3
Corporate profits taxes- total	6.3	9.6
SOE	0.9	6.0
Collective enterprises	11.7	1.6
Foreign-funded enterprises	35.3	2.0
Personal income taxes	41.5	3.9

Note: Value-added taxes are levied primarily on industry while business taxes are levied on revenue of service and some other tertiary activities.
Source: *China Statistical Yearbook*, 2000.

these factors, together with changes in tax provisions that authorities are now contemplating, could raise tax revenues by a further several percentage points of GDP over the next five to ten years.[44]

Improvements in the tax structure and administration and better mechanisms for budget planning, formulation, and monitoring would also help to increase tax revenues and to maximise their benefits. The potential gains from better collection and compliance underscore the pay off from devoting resources to improvement of the efficiency of the tax administration. Central government authorities are consolidating numerous extra-budget fees imposed by local governments into a more coherent and efficient system of taxes that are more even across jurisdictions. Authorities are also considering other changes in the tax system, including a phased convergence of the tax treatment of foreign and domestic enterprises, that have the potential to raise substantial revenues and which are ultimately needed to establish a more level playing field among enterprises.

Effective mechanisms for planning, formulating, and monitoring the government's budget are also essential to ensure that revenues are efficiently used. The budget is typically the single most important overall government-planning tool in OECD countries but is much less important in China. Government authorities endorse the need for budget reform and are planning to establish a Treasury Single Account to monitor outlays and resources of government organs. This will provide essential institutions for more advanced reforms. However, capabilities to formulate comprehensive budgets that, 1) include all government revenues

© OECD 2002

and expenditures, 2) are based on realistic forecasts of revenues and expenditures, and 3) are embedded in a multi-year planning context, are still some way off.

The second key objective is to *establish a sustainable system of pension and other social benefits*. Even with no change in the present limited coverage, benefits will rise more rapidly than GDP as a result of population ageing. Extension of social benefits to the nearly 80 per cent of workers that are not now covered will not be feasible at current pension benefit rates, which are quite generous by international standards (Table 8). However, in contrast to the situation that has faced some OECD countries, the authorities are not yet locked into untenably high benefit rates.

Significant progress has been made in providing the institutional basis for sharing the financing of social benefits. A three-tier pension system has been established along lines recommended by the OECD and the World Bank. The government is directly responsible for the first tier, which is a defined benefit plan financed by a payroll tax and intended to cover one-third of targeted pension benefits.[45] The remaining two-thirds will be supplied by second and third (voluntary) tier defined contribution plans. The financing of health care benefits has been established on a similar basis.

Recent reforms have gone part of the way toward reducing future pension benefits and the new pension system provides the basis for further reductions over time to levels that are sustainable.[46] The challenge in the medium term is to manage the transition between the presently high benefits promised under the first tier to current middle-aged and older workers and the lower benefits that younger workers will receive. Currently, younger workers in the formal sector are effectively taxed to pay for the higher benefits to those nearing retirement, which creates incentives to work in the uncovered informal sector. These disincentives could be reduced by allowing lower contribution rates for younger or lower paid workers, while making up for the loss of payroll contributions out of other revenues. There is also a need to start preparations for organising social insurance for rural workers. This might be done by initially extending coverage with lower benefit and contribution rates to selected agricultural areas bordering the cities, with a view to gradually raising the rates over time.

The third objective is to *contain future non-performing loans and so avoid the need for another financial system cleanup after the one that needs to be undertaken now*. This is absolutely essential: the possibility that new non-performing loans will not be adequately contained is probably the single greatest risk to fiscal sustainability in China. Thus financial reforms to ensure that financial institutions have the incentives and capabilities to maintain rigorous lending standards and manage risk are critical to maintaining sound public finances.

© OECD 2002

Table 8. **China's pension system compared with selected regions in the world**
(China in 1999 compared with regional averages in the mid-1990s)

Region	Participation as share of labour force (%)	Contributions as ratio to wages (%)		Average income replacement ratio (%)	Average pension as per cent of GDP per capita	Pension spending as per cent of GDP
		Pensions	All social insurance			
China (1999)	**18**[1]	**25**[2]	**30**[3]	**77**[2]	**99**[2]	**3**
OECD	**90**	**19**	**34**	**38**	**54**	**10**
Range	79-98	6-35	14-57	25-49	23-98	5-15
Asia and the Pacific	**26**	**14**	**17**	**na**	**na**	**1**
Range	3-73	3-40	4-46	*na*	*na*	0-3
Central and Eastern Europe[4]	**66**	**22**	**31**	**44**	**39**	**7**
Range	32-97	20-45	24-61	24-69	13-92	2-14
North Africa and Middle East	**41**	**13**	**23**	**55**	**71**	**3**
Range	30-82	3-27	13-48	36-78	22-144	0-6
Sub-Saharan Africa	**6**	**10**	**17**	**na**	**135**	**1**
Range	1-18	3-24	6-33	na	40-207	0-3
Latin America and Caribbean	**33**	**12**	**21**	**39**	**50**	**3**
Range	11-82	3-29	8-46	13-64	26-64	0-13

1. The regular urban pension system and that for civil servants.
2. The regular urban pension system. N.B. employee contribution rates increased every year 1997-2001.
3. Approximate national average.
4. Including the former Soviet Union.

Source: The Table is adapted from Chapter 16, Table 16.8, which gives further details. Figures are based on calculations using World Bank data.

© OECD 2002

Conditions for fiscal sustainability:

- ***Raise tax revenues sufficiently to accommodate increased needs for spending on development.***
- ***Establish sustainable benefit levels for social insurance programmes.***
- ***Contain future non-performing loans by sustaining sound lending standards***

Reforming central-local government fiscal relations[47]

China's fiscal system is relatively decentralised, with local governments accounting for 71 per cent of government expenditure. Since the major reform of central-government fiscal relations in 1994, the VAT, business, personal and other on-budget taxes have been subject to explicit revenue-sharing formulae. Expenditure responsibilities are also explicitly divided, with the central government responsible for national defence while local governments have the main responsibility for education, agriculture, and most social welfare payments. Transfers between the central and local government are also relatively large, accounting for nearly 42 per cent of central government revenues and nearly 5 per cent of GDP.

Despite this decentralisation, many local governments are starved for revenues to meet local needs. While due partly to the low level of tax revenues for government as a whole, the scarcity at the local level is aggravated by the current fiscal federalism system. The system has also resulted in large disparities among richer and poorer regions. *Per-capita* government expenditure in Shanghai is six to eight times greater than in most central and western provinces; budget revenues relative to local GDP are two to three times higher on the coast than in most western provinces. The fiscal system therefore accentuates the imbalances and lack of integration among regions.

One of the underlying causes of these problems is the fact that expenditures are more decentralised than tax revenues. Sub-national governments – provincial governments and the local levels subject to their jurisdiction, receive about 55 per cent of total tax revenues, but these account for less than half of their spending, with the remainder coming from extra-budget funds and from transfers from the central government. The expenditures assigned to sub-national government are among the most rapidly growing components of overall government spending. They are also the areas where the need for further increases is greatest. Sub-national governments are mainly responsible for supporting SOE workers displaced by labour shedding and for making up shortfalls in contributions to pay for

© OECD 2002

social welfare benefits. Sub-national governments have little (sanctioned) flexibility in setting the criteria for spending or in determining the rates even on those taxes assigned entirely to them. Indeed, under-funded mandates from the central government have added to the pressures on local finances in recent years. Local governments' flexibility, even to smooth out fluctuations in their revenue, is limited by the requirement that their budget be balanced each fiscal year. The squeeze on sub-national revenues is further heightened by inefficiencies in spending, such as the maintenance of an excessive number of government staff.

A second problem lies with the central-local government transfer mechanism. This mechanism is based in part on the earlier system in which transfers to a province were related to its success in raising revenues above a targeted base amount. Partly as a result, the transfer system does not appreciably offset discrepancies between the tax bases of rich and poor provinces. A third problem lies with the inefficient distribution of revenues between provincial governments and their local governments. This is attributable in part to the influence of political and other non-commercial considerations, and in part to the lack of formal national criteria governing the allocation.

Establishment of a better balance between local government resources and their spending is a key objective of broader fiscal reforms. Reform of central-local government fiscal relations is important to reduce the incentives for regional protectionism and other distorting resource extraction by local governments, and to improve regional integration. OECD experiences suggest that the appropriate division of responsibilities among various levels of governments to meet these objectives depends heavily on country circumstances, in particular the capabilities and incentives of the various levels of government, and may have to change over time.[48] However the overall objectives of the reforms should be, first, to bring tax revenues of sub-national governments in to line with their expenditure needs. This is likely to require both review of the current assignment of tax revenues and expenditure responsibilities and reform of the transfer mechanism. The second objective is to improve revenue and expenditure within provinces by setting clearer standards at the national level and by giving provinces more flexibility in administering their finances, including some ability to set rates on local taxes and to borrow to meet short-term liquidity needs.

Improving the flexibility of macroeconomic policy instruments[49]

The diverse forces that will impact China's economy from trade and investment liberalisation and the restructuring of the domestic real economy will place heavy demands on China's macroeconomic policy instruments. As the earlier discussion suggests, macroeconomic policy will need to be able to support higher real GDP growth in order to reduce the current slack in labour markets – once

© OECD 2002

structural problems have been alleviated enough to allow higher growth without igniting inflation. The exchange rate necessary to maintain China's external balance may also change, but the amount and direction cannot be predicted in advance. The study points to three priority objectives for improving the effectiveness and flexibility of China's macroeconomic policy instruments to deal with these prospective changes.

The first is to *improve the effectiveness of monetary policy in managing aggregate demand* so that the burden does not fall disproportionately on fiscal policy, as is now the case. Important steps have been taken in recent years toward developing instruments for "indirect" monetary policy management of domestic credit. At least for the medium term, the next challenge is largely one of strengthening monetary policy transmission mechanisms. One important source of the weakness in the transmission mechanisms – the poor financial conditions of enterprises and of banks that together are responsible for the present credit crunch – is likely to take some time to fully remedy.

However, much progress could be made in the near term on two other important steps. The first is to deregulate interest rates on bank loans and on large deposits. Interest rates in the inter-bank market have already been freed and authorities have announced plans to liberalise bank loan (and some deposit) rates within three years.[50] Acceleration in this schedule would be desirable. The current restriction on bank loan rates limits the ability of central bank operating instruments to control the effective cost of credit to final borrowers. The second step is to improve the flexibility of the money markets. While development of the money markets is also a longer process, broadening access to the market and liberalising the positions permitted to participants would help to distribute the effects of monetary policy changes more broadly and evenly.

A second objective is to *accelerate the development of the government bond market* in order to accommodate the large increase in government debt that is likely to be needed over the next several years. The current government bond markets are limited by their segmentation into two tiers, the stock market and inter-bank market, low liquidity in both the primary and secondary markets, and by disincentives to active trading. Banks are the largest holders of government bonds but are only able to trade in the interbank market (since they have been banned from the stock exchanges), and tend to follow a buy and hold strategy encouraged by the positive gap between bond interest rates and bank loan rates. Integration of the two tiers would probably be the most effective step in the near-term to improve the liquidity and breadth of the market. As the stock of debt grows, it will be increasingly important to broaden access by domestic institutional investors, and, at a suitable point, to allow foreigners to purchase government bonds. Development of the money market and liberalisation of bank loan

© OECD 2002

rates is also important to bond market development, for example to help securities dealers to fund inventories of government bonds.[51]

The third objective, and the most difficult challenge, is *to progressively increase the flexibility of the exchange rate and capital control regimes*. The Chinese authorities have been considering technical means in the near-term to make exchange rate management more flexible, notably by widening the band within which the rate is allowed to vary. However, greater flexibility is likely to be needed beyond the near term to allow the nominal exchange rate to vary in line with the requirements of external balance while avoiding the speculative disruptions that have often accompanied adjustable parity regimes in the past. Ultimately, a floating exchange rate regime may well be most suitable to China's conditions, in part because of the ability it will allow for more independent monetary policy once the capital account is liberalised. Capital account liberalisation, however, is essential to ensure that the foreign exchange market is sufficiently broad and efficient to determine a price for the domestic currency that is in line with its underlying competitiveness. Progressive liberalisation of the capital account will also be needed to allow domestic businesses sufficient access to international financial markets as trade and investment liberalisation progresses, and to help spur the development of domestic financial markets.

Identifying the concrete steps needed to balance these considerations is very difficult. Recent international experience has graphically illustrated the risk to macroeconomic stability posed by capital account liberalisation when domestic financial markets are insufficiently developed or subject to distortiums. The risks of premature liberalisation are now especially great in China because of the poor financial conditions of enterprises and financial institutions, weak corporate governance, and the incomplete development of the financial supervisory and regulatory system. However, delay in liberalising the capital account also involves a cost, since it limits the degree to which the exchange rate regime can be made more flexible as well as the potential benefits of liberalised capital flows to the domestic economy.

In the near term, the stability afforded by the present exchange rate regime is probably beneficial to China's economy but there is also a need to establish a foundation for greater flexibility in the future. To this end, it would be useful to partially relax existing capital controls over the next several years to give enterprises more flexible access to foreign exchange and to create a broader and more efficient foreign exchange market. Once supervisory mechanisms have been adequately strengthened, further relaxation of controls on portfolio capital flows, starting with equity and government bond markets, would be useful.

© OECD 2002

Creating the framework for a market-based regulatory system[52]

Regulatory reform is a major part of the policy effort to realise the full benefits of trade and investment liberalisation. Establishment of the conditions needed to integrate the internal economy and the frameworks for market functioning is a process involving new regulation in some areas, deregulation in many others, and revised regulation nearly everywhere. The overall objective is to focus regulation on establishing and enforcing the rules and processes for effective market functioning, rather than on resource extraction or government-directed resource allocation.

One of the most basic lessons OECD countries have learned from their experiences over the past fifty years is that regulation is not simply a collection of laws and regulations in individual areas but a process in its own right. To be fully effective, the regulatory process, and not simply its individual components, needs to be based on a comprehensive and coherent long-term framework with clearly defined priorities and strategies. There is a growing body of evidence that a coherent regulatory process can yield significant economic benefits in terms of lower costs to business, greater choices for consumers, improved innovative capacity, and other gains.

The potential benefits of a comprehensive regulatory framework are especially great for China for at least three reasons:

- First, it would help to level the playing field for domestic firms in competing with foreign enterprises that benefit from a coherent regulatory framework in their own countries.
- Second, a comprehensive framework is needed to harmonise regulatory policies that up to now have largely been developed sector by sector, or driven by outside commitments such as those under WTO. It would also help to improve co-ordination, consistency, and accountability in the regulatory efforts of the myriad government agencies and levels that too often operate in isolation, and sometimes at cross-purposes, in China.
- Third, an overall regulatory framework can contribute to China's effort to establish a market economy by providing a more rigorous basis for balancing purely economic objectives with other social values, such as equity and the need to provide support to those displaced by economic transformation.

OECD experience, and the work of OECD experts with non-member countries, underscore that there is no single blueprint for an effective regulatory framework that is applicable to all. The appropriate institutions and strategies depend heavily on the traditions and circumstances of each individual economy. However, OECD experiences suggest several guiding principles. The first is the need to develop the institutional structures within government for regulatory planning, co-ordination,

© OECD 2002

and accountability across all its components and levels. Most OECD governments now have central regulatory co-ordination agencies with government-wide scope. In the United States, for example, the Office of Management and Budget provides this co-ordinating role. China presently does not have such a function, but several current organs reporting directly to the State Council have more limited co-ordination roles that could serve as the basis for development of a broader regulatory co-ordinating body. Development of such a capability could help greatly to overcome administrative blockages and delays in mandated reforms and to achieve a clearer definition of responsibilities for particular regulatory areas across government agencies. Over a longer period, a regulatory co-ordinating body could serve as a catalyst for more fundamental rationalisation of regulatory policies that are now carried out by numerous bodies.

A second principle is that regulatory authorities need to have tools to objectively evaluate the impact of proposed policies and the trade-offs they involve. Such tools are particularly important when, as in China, developing markets and institutions are subject to distortions that increase the risk that poorly designed regulations will have perverse effects. In China, policy evaluation is most often carried out through consultations with local government officials, the testing of certain policies at selected local levels before nationwide implementation,[53] and by commissioning government and academic think tanks to develop policy options and assessments of the impact of proposed actions. However, more formal tools that could be applied directly by government agencies are likely to be needed as regulatory policy develops. In OECD countries, competition policy is often used to evaluate not only the impact of particular regulations on competition but also their trade-offs in terms of efficiency, environmental standards, and other broader goals. The regulatory framework needs to explicitly require the use of such tools by regulatory agencies and to specify their applicability and priority in particular areas.

Transparency is the third requirement of an effective regulatory framework and is the area where China's regulatory system most lags behind that of OECD countries. Transparency is essential to all phases of the regulatory process, from formulation, to implementation, and to ongoing administration. Transparency rests first on the principle that those regulated, as well as the general public, need to be accurately and thoroughly informed about regulatory rules and their changes. Public knowledge of the rules is necessary not only for those regulated, but also to ensure that government agencies at all levels are fully aware of their obligations, to ensure accountability, and to prevent capture of regulatory organs by special interests. Disclosure of regulations also serves as a commitment by regulatory authorities to the public that can help to buttress their credibility. Efforts to inform the public need to go beyond purely formal but *ad hoc* means (such as announcement in the speech of a senior official) to include a pro-active effort to inform the public through channels that can be easily accessed.

© OECD 2002

Box 4. Priorities for strengthening the government's capabilities to foster economic development

Problem	Priority objectives	Some suggested steps
Public finances are insufficient to adequately meet development needs while maintaining fiscal sustainability	Bolster the capacity of the fiscal system by raising revenues relative to GDP, completing the establishment of a financially viable system of social benefits, and contain further non-performing loans	*a*) In the medium term, continue to improve tax collection and compliance; reform tax provisions to reduce distortions; and strengthen public management of the budget *b*) Over a longer period, reduce pension benefit rates to viable levels as coverage is extended
Local government fiscal resources are insufficient to meet their responsibilities and very unevenly distributed	Establish a better balance between local government resources and expenditure responsibilities	*a*) In the near term, review current assignment of revenue and expenditure responsibilities *b*) Over a longer period, reform the transfer mechanism to better direct funds on the basis of need; and establish criteria for a more efficient allocation of fiscal resources within provinces
Macroeconomic policy instruments are insufficiently flexible	Bolster the effectiveness of monetary policy instruments; accelerate the development of the government bond market, and move toward greater flexibility in the exchange rate and capital control regimes over time	*a*) Liberalise bank loan rates in the near term and remove restrictions that inhibit the money and government bond markets *b*) Over the longer term, liberalise the capital account and exchange rate regimes in line with development of domestic financial markets and improvements in financial discipline and supervision
The regulatory framework needs to be better aligned with the needs of an integrated market economy	Develop a comprehensive government-wide regulatory framework in which the government is an arms-length formulator and arbiter of rules for the market	*a*) In the near term, develop bodies to co-ordinate regulatory policy for the government as a whole *b*) Continue efforts to improve transparency and develop explicit tools to evaluate regulatory impacts

© OECD 2002

Finally, an effective regulatory system requires strong enforcement mechanisms that are consistent with the rule of law. Regulatory enforcement in China is decentralised to lower government levels to a greater extent than in most OECD countries. Regulatory authorities at these levels are hampered by interference from local governments are prone to capture by special interests, and often lack effective sanctions for violators. Operating without clear mandates or guidelines from the central government, local regulation is often excessive and intrusive. OECD countries typically have enacted explicit laws to clarify the scope of regulators and sanction abuses. The study suggests that China could build on several existing administrative laws to develop a more effective legal framework to achieve the same goals.

Conclusions

Collectively, the chapters of this study highlight the impressive progress China has made in recent years to prepare for further integration into the world economy. In nearly all the areas examined, the authorities have been moving in the direction needed to deal with inherited problems and to foster conditions to allow the benefits of trade and investment liberalisation to be realised. The chapters highlight areas where, based on OECD experiences and perspectives, further changes are likely to be needed to reinforce policies now underway or planned, and to improve prospects for achieving China's economic development objectives.

Although China has already opened considerably to international markets, the potential gains from further trade and investment liberalisation are very great. However, as the individual chapters illustrate, realisation of these gains is neither inevitable nor automatic, and depends crucially on progress on domestic economic reforms. Trade and investment liberalisation does not radically alter the priorities for domestic economic reforms, but it does make some steps all the more urgent.

The overall conclusion that emerges from the study is that China's development has now reached a stage that calls for a somewhat different emphasis in reforms from that prevailing earlier. Past policies to develop individual segments of the economy were based in part on the limited development of markets and their supporting mechanisms in the early stages of the reform era. As the scope for market forces has progressively increased and development has advanced, the administrative distinctions among these segments have come to have less and less economic meaning. Thus the problems and challenges of SOE and non-state enterprises are becoming more and more similar; conditions in the rural economy now depend more on national economic developments than on developments specific to the agriculture sector or rural industries themselves. Problems in individual

© OECD 2002

areas and the policies needed to deal with them have become increasingly interdependent. As a result, the benefits to separate development of preferred sectors have reached sharply diminishing returns, and the risk that they will impose distortions that will be counter-productive for the overall economy has increased. Rather than seeking to replicate past policies, future policies need to be based on their underlying lessons, the most important of which is that allowing greater scope for market forces is the key to successful development.

Future economic reforms need to continue and broaden the trend in recent years toward measures with economy wide scope, focused on two essential objectives. The first is to foster the integration of the domestic economy in order to realise the benefits of trade and investment liberalisation and to sustain China's development over the longer term. As underscored by the high degree of internal integration of the United States economy, and the strenuous efforts the European Community has been making to achieve it to a comparable degree, internal integration is essential to the development of an advanced continental economy. Domestic integration in China is essential to achieving better utilisation of labour and other resources as well as to ensure that resources are efficiently employed in the future. Integration of the domestic economy involves the elimination of internal barriers to mobility in factor and product markets, creation of a more level playing field among enterprises and other economic segments, and greater scope for market forces in certain areas. Integration among China's regions, and between rural and urban areas, needs to become a major priority, not simply to improve equity, but to sustain the development of the economy as a whole. Development of interior provinces is likely to have to depart somewhat from the model suggested by China's coastal development, with the emphasis on integration with the rest of the country and improvement in the local business environment, rather than on special zones or other government preferences, as the keys to success.

Success in integrating the domestic economy also depends on achievement of a second key objective, which is to strengthen the framework conditions necessary for efficient market functioning. This is an ongoing process that continues even in the most advanced economies. However, in developing countries such as China, limited institutional development and the distortions left by central planning make framework reforms a critical priority. The study has identified five priorities for these reforms. These are to clarify property rights and strengthen exit mechanisms so that state-owned as well as other assets can be allocated to their most efficient uses; to improve competition and, in the process, break down regional and other protectionist barriers; to bolster enterprise governance by making managers and their boards more independent and accountable while strengthening external discipline; to buttress the powers and capabilities of financial supervisory authorities; and to underpin reforms generally by improving the independence and enforcement capabilities of the judiciary. While likely to take some time to complete improvement in

© OECD 2002

framework conditions needs to be given high priority in the near and medium term since the adjustments entailed by trade and investment liberalisation are likely to create incentives to interfere with competition and impose other distortions to market functioning in order to protect incumbent interests.

More than in the past, success in achieving these objectives will require co-ordinated policies on a broad range of fronts that takes account of the increasing interdependence among current problems. At the same time, policies need to be carefully sequenced in order to establish the pre-conditions for subsequent reforms. In this regard, measures to break through the vicious circles that are blocking progress on broader reforms take on a particularly high near-term priority. Timely restoration of financial system solvency is important *not* because it will be sufficient by itself but because international experience suggests it is necessary to allow broader financial and real sector reforms to proceed. Government imposed and other obstacles to enterprise restructuring need to be removed as soon as possible if the business sector is to keep up with the imperatives that will come with trade and investment liberalisation. And government financial resources need to be bolstered in order to provide the support needed to facilitate these and other reforms that will need to be undertaken in the medium term.

Finally, China's government will need to continue to play a key role in the economic reform process. The chapters identify measures to bolster public finances, reform central-local government finances, improve the effectiveness of macroeconomic policy instruments, and develop a more comprehensive regulatory policy framework in order to improve the capabilities of the government to support reforms. These changes point to a broader need to re-orient the role of the government in the economy that is not unique to China. Public ownership of enterprises, the use of tax, regulatory, and other policies to influence resource allocation, and reliance on credit rationing and other direct interventions in macroeconomic policy were much more common in OECD countries during the 1950s and 1960s than they are now. Public governance in OECD countries has since evolved toward a more effective framework based on the following principles. The task of public finances is to extract sufficient resources to achieve the government's objectives through means that minimise distortions to market forces. The task of macroeconomic policy is to sustain internal and external balance in the economy through market-based policy instruments. And the task of government regulation, including regulatory reform, is to formulate, enact, and enforce rules to sustain competition and other framework conditions needed for market functioning. With this evolution, has come a need to rationalise government structures and capabilities in order to ensure that policies are adequately co-ordinated, understood by those they affect, and are carried out in a mutually reinforcing and consistent manner over time. Public governance in China is already moving in this direction and will need to continue to do so as the domestic economy develops and integration with the outside world proceeds.

© OECD 2002

Notes

1. Barry Naughton (1995), *Growing out of the plan: Chinese economic reform, 1978-93*, Cambridge University Press.
2. This section is based mainly on Chapters 1-3 on agriculture and the rural sector.
3. Grains account for nearly two-thirds of total cultivated land. As throughout the reform period, the government establishes procurement prices and delivery quotas for major grains, including wheat, corn, and rice, and controls grain marketing, while allowing farmers to sell their surplus above the quota in the open market. The Governors' Grain Bag Responsibility System (GGBRS) introduced in 1995 sought to increase production by raising prices to farmers. The result has been led to rising surpluses. Despite progressive reduction in support prices in recent years, the gap between procurement and market prices has continued to widen. The grain procurement system is not covered by China's WTO agreement but is likely to become increasingly expensive to maintain once the domestic market is opened to lower cost imports from abroad.
4. REs, as the term is used in this synthesis, include all rural non-agricultural enterprises, including single owner and other private firms. This term is equivalent to TVEs as they are defined in Chapters 1-3. TVEs are sometimes defined more narrowly as rural collective enterprises; these account for most rural industrial output.
5. See the simulations discussed in Chapter 4 on industry implications and in Annex 2.
6. This sub-section is based on Chapters 4-6 on industry issues and Chapter 10 on foreign direct investment.
7. China ranked only eighth among developing country recipients of foreign direct investment in 1999. Studies cited in Chapter 10 on foreign direct investment suggest that China does not outperform other developing countries on average once its size and other characteristics are taken into account.
8. Empirical evidence on the impact of trade and investment liberalisation on China's industries is reviewed in Annex 2.
9. This section is based on Chapter 7 on banking, Chapter 8 on insurance, Chapter 14 on priorities for the financial system and financial regulatory policy, and Chapter 15 on capital market development.
10. China's financial system is relatively large, as measured by the ratio of domestic credit to GDP, compared to countries of comparable development. (See Chapter 14 on financial system priorities, Figure 4).
11. As mentioned in Chapter 7 on the banking sector, a recent People's Bank of China survey indicates that a significantly higher portion of bank lending goes indirectly to non-state entities than is apparent from official figures on their direct lending. This pattern is indicative of the importance of informal credit channels in China. However the degree

© OECD 2002

to which non-state non-financial businesses are recipients of these indirect funds is unclear. Much of the indirect financing probably goes through informal financial channels into the stock market or other investments that banks are not allowed to engage in directly.

12. Foreign banks' ability to lend foreign currency will be constrained by the underdeveloped domestic interbank market and foreign exchange and other regulatory constraints not covered by WTO accession. See Chapter 7.
13. See Chapter 22 on macroeconomic issues.
14. China's trade (merchandise exports plus imports) to GDP was 38 per cent of GDP in 1999, compared to 26 per cent for the Euro area, 19 per cent for the United States, and 17 per cent for Japan. China ranks third among the five largest developing countries by this measure, behind Russia and Indonesia but substantially above Brazil and India.
15. China's domestically held public debt is about 22 per cent of GDP.
16. See the estimates discussed in Chapter 14.
17. Studies reviewed in Annex 2 suggest that real GDP growth could be boosted by an amount ranging from virtually negligible to as much as 0.5 per cent annually through 2010. The estimated effects on employment are small.
18. See Chapter 21 on regional issues.
19. See Chapters 2-3 on the rural sector and Chapter 16 on labour market and social policies.
20. See Chapter 16, on labour market and social policies.
21. See Chapter 17 on environmental issues and Chapter 1 on the agricultural sector.
22. See Chapter 1, concluding section.
23. See Chapters 4-6 on industry implications.
24. See Chapters 7 and 8 on the banking and insurance sectors, respectively, Chapter 14 on financial system priorities, and Chapter 15 on capital markets.
25. Partial clean-ups that simply reduce the amount of negative capital tend to have little impact on internal incentives to maintain prudential standards or to monitor loan contracts. See Aghion, Philippe, Olivier Jean Blanchard, and Wendy Carlin (1994), "*The economics of enterprise restructuring in Central and Eastern Europe*", *Centre for Economic Policy Research Discussion Paper* No. 1058.
26. Chapter 14 on priorities for financial system development presents rough illustrative calculations suggesting that the cost to China's government of a thorough clean up in the near-term could range between 30 and 60 per cent of GDP, depending on the true extent of non-performing loans, the recovery rate, and other circumstances. This range is comparable to the costs incurred by other developing countries that have undergone severe banking crises. The cost to China's government could be lower if the clean up were less comprehensive, or authorities were to rely substantially on the banks to "grow out" of their problems, but as argued in the text and in the chapters on the financial system, this is a risky strategy that could easily lead to greater costs in the future.
27. See Chapter 21 on regional economic issues.
28. The issues summarised in this and the following sub-section are discussed in detail in Chapter 13 on enterprise governance issues.

© OECD 2002

29. A basic step was taken in 1993 with the enactment of the Company Law providing for the establishment of legally autonomous limited liability and joint-stock companies, and specifying the rights of shareholders, and powers of managers and their boards of directors and supervisors. The company law does not cover all types of enterprises. Collective enterprises are subject to an earlier law. Private enterprises were not officially sanctioned until 1998 and are still subject to ambiguities about their legitimate scope.
30. Chinese authorities, including the Chairman of the China Securities Regulatory Commission, have explicitly stated that they regard the OECD Principles on Corporate Governance as the international benchmark in this area.
31. See the *Economist* article cited in Chapter 13 on enterprise governance.
32. Discipline is further constrained by the limited rights of minority shareholders.
33. As noted in Chapter 4, enterprise governance has improved most in sectors that are competitive.
34. Cyril Lin, *Corporate governance in China* (2000).
35. The decentralisation of state administration has effectively increased the number of "owners". Creation of separate asset management companies has not resolved this problem because the companies tend to function very similarly to the line government agencies from which they are typically derived. The separation of SOEs from their controlling line agencies may have had the perverse effect of making it easier for other government entities to interfere in their operations.
36. This section is based on Chapter 12 on competition law and policy but also draws on Chapter 11, on regulatory reform.
37. Overt barriers to product market competition are focused on a few products, such as automobiles and beer, and have been declining as a result of central government crackdowns.
38. These amount to RMB 300 000, or US$36 000, in retail trade and RMB 500 000 (US$60 000) in wholesale trade and manufacturing. See Chapter 13 on corporate governance.
39. See Chapter 14, the section on regulatory/supervisory policies, for further discussion of these issues.
40. This power now lies with the Ministry of Finance.
41. The issues for this sub-section are discussed in detail in Chapters 16 (section on pensions), 17 (public budget management) and 18 (tax policies), as well as Chapter 22 on macroeconomic implications.
42. See Nicolas Lardy (2000), "Fiscal sustainability: between a rock and hard place", *China Economic Quarterly*.
43. A 1997 study by the World Bank estimated that only 70 per cent of the VAT due to authorities was actually collected and there seems to have been only limited improvement since that date. See, World Bank, *China* 2020 (1997).
44. See Chapter 22 on macroeconomic policy issues and Chapter 18 on tax policies.
45. Under current policy the first tier benefit replaces 20 per cent of a worker's average wage, although changes now being considered could raise this to 30 per cent.
46. Calculations developed in Chapter 16 suggest that a 20 per cent replacement rate in the first tier could be financed by a payroll tax of 10 per cent, even with the expected rise in the dependency ratio.

© OECD 2002

47. Further discussion of these issues can be found in Chapter 20 on central-local government fiscal relations.
48. This conclusion is further supported by recent Secretariat economic surveys of Russia and Brazil. See the chapters on central-local government relations in the OECD *Economic Surveys* for Russia (2001) and Brazil (2001).
49. These issues are discussed in detail in Chapter 22.
50. As with other policies, the exact timetable implicit in official announcements is not entirely clear, but three years from the time this plan was first stated would be in 2003.
51. As discussed in Chapter 15 on capital markets, China could improve the liquidity and depth of the government bond market by adopting techniques already used in major markets, such as standardising terms on bond issues, consolidating issues into a limited number of categories, and establishing a pre-announced schedule of regular issues.
52. These issues are discussed in Chapter 11 on regulatory policy; see also the portion of Chapter 12 on competition policy.
53. An example is the housing reform now applying nation-wide but which was first tested for several years in Shanghai.

© OECD 2002

OECD/CCNM Publications on China

Published in 2001

- China's Agriculture in the International Trading System
  Code 142001111P ISBN 92-64-18682-4
- Business Cycles and Cyclical Indicators
  Jointly published by the OECD Statistics Directorate, the Centre for Co-operation with Non-Members and the National Bureau of Statistics of The People's Republic of China (NBS)
- Research of Methodological Issues on National Accounts (Series No. 4)
  Jointly published by the OECD Statistics Directorate and the National Bureau of Statistics of The People's Republic of China (NBS)

Published in 2000

- National Accounts for China – Sources and Methods
  Code 142000281P1, ISBN 92-64-18550-X
- Reforming China's Enterprises
  Code 112000171P1, ISBN 92-64-17697-7
- Réussir la réforme des entreprises en Chine
  Code 112000172P1, ISBN 92-64-27697-1
  (also in Chinese)
- The Agro-food Processing Sector in China – Developments and Policy Challenges
  Code 142000011P1, ISBN 92-64-17179-7

Published in 1999

- Agriculture in China and OECD Countries – Past Policies and Future Challenges
  Code 141999071P1, ISBN 92-64-17094-4
- Environmental Taxes – Recent Developments in China and OECD countries
  Code 971999071P1, ISBN 92-64-17092-8

© OECD 2002

- Research of Methodological Issues on National Accounts (Series No. 3)
  Jointly published by the OECD Statistics Directorate and the National Bureau of Statistics of The People's Republic of China (NBS) Published in 1997
- Agricultural Policies in China
  Code 511997111P1, ISBN 92-64 15562-7
- Politiques agricoles en Chine
  Code 511997112P1, ISBN 92-64-25562-1
- Applying Market-based Instruments to Environmental Policies in China and OECD Countries
  Code 971997171P1, ISBN 92-64-15618-6
- Les instruments économiques des politiques d'environnement en Chine et dans les pays de l'OCDE
  Code 971997172P1, ISBN 92-64-25618-0
- Research of Methodological Issues on National Accounts (Series No. 2)
  Jointly published by the OECD Statistics Directorate and the National Bureau of Statistics of The People's Republic of China (NBS)

© OECD 2002

OECD PUBLICATIONS, 2, rue André-Pascal, 75775 PARIS CEDEX 16
PRINTED IN FRANCE
(14 2002 05 1P) ISBN 92-64-19708-7 – No. 52389 2002